# TRANS
# IN
# TRANSITION

Research by the Energy and Environmental Programme is supported by generous contributions of finance and professional advice from the following organizations:

AEA Technology · Amerada Hess · Arthur D Little
Ashland Oil · British Coal · British Nuclear Fuels
British Petroleum · European Commission
Department of Trade and Industry · Eastern Electricity
Enterprise Oil · ENRON Europe · Exxon · LASMO
Mobil · National Grid · National Power · Nuclear Electric
Overseas Development Administration · PowerGen
Saudi Aramco · Shell · Statoil · Texaco · Total
Tokyo Electric Power Company

# TRANSPORT
# IN
# TRANSITION

## LESSONS FROM THE HISTORY OF ENERGY

## STEPHEN PEAKE

THE ROYAL INSTITUTE OF
INTERNATIONAL AFFAIRS
Energy and Environmental Programme

EARTHSCAN
Earthscan Publications Ltd, London

First published in Great Britain in 1994 by
Earthscan Publications Ltd, 120 Pentonville Road, London N1 9JN and
Royal Institute of International Affairs, 10 St James's Square, London SW1Y 4LE

Distributed in North America by
The Brookings Institution, 1775 Massachusetts Avenue NW,
Washington DC 20036-2188

ISBN 1 85383 209 X

Earthscan Publications Limited is an editorially independent subsidiary of Kogan Page
Limited and publishes in association with the International Institute of Environment and
Development and the World Wide Fund for Nature.

Printed and bound by Biddles Limited, Guildford and King's Lynn
Cover by Elaine Marriott

# Contents

**Boxes**

# About the Author

Stephen Peake is a Research Fellow with the Energy and Environmental Programme at the Royal Institute of International Affairs, specializing in cross-sector transport, energy and environmental research. Dr Peake holds a degree in Physics from the University of Sussex, and a Ph.D in Management Studies from the University of Cambridge. He has worked as a Research Associate in the field of environmental management and auditing and is co-author of papers in several international journals.

# Acknowledgements

This research began in October 1989, when I was awarded a Science and Engineering Research Council post-graduate studentship at the Management Studies Group in the Department of Engineering at the University of Cambridge. First thanks must go to my family, Sarah and Charlie, for their patience and love during what has since been a busy time for us all. Thank you to the Council for their financial support, to the members of the Management Studies Group, and to Professor Stephen Watson. I would like to give special thanks to a good friend, Dr Chris Hope, for his generous guidance and support in supervising the original project. Over the past five years I have sought the help and views of many people sharing cross-interests in the energy and transport sectors. Thanks in particular to Professor John Chesshire at the University of Sussex, Professor Richard Eden at the University of Cambridge, Dr Phil Goodwin at the University of Oxford, Dr Mayer Hillman of the Policy Studies Institute, London, and Dr Alan Pearman at the University of Leeds for their encouragement, ideas and comments. Thanks also to Roger Rainbow, Phil Elliot and Roger Booth for their help and advice in a number of areas during my secondment in late 1993 to Group Planning, Shell International, London.

Turning what started its life as a doctoral dissertation into this report has been a rewarding journey. Many refinements to the original ideas have taken place during my Fellowship with the Energy and Environmental Programme. The study group for the final report was especially helpful. Thank you to all who took part, and to Malcolm Fergusson, Stephen Joseph, Professor Chris Nash, Dr Lee Schipper, and Professor John Surrey who made detailed comments and criticisms on the final draft. I am grateful to all my colleagues at Chatham House and the Energy and Environmental Programme, with thanks in particular to Dr Michael Grubb for his diligent guidance and careful support, to Walt Patterson, Dr Oliver Sparrow and Matthew Tickle. I am particularly grateful to Nicole Dando for managing the project splendidly.

*July 1994*                                                         Stephen Peake

# Summary and Conclusions

Perception of the full costs of coping with transport demand is growing. Increasing transport energy demands, atmospheric pollution, congestion, health disorders, and social problems challenge the feasibility and wisdom of meeting unbounded transport growth with purely technological palliatives. Both the real impacts of actual transport increases and the psychological effects of growth projections are focusing minds on the prospect of a fundamental transition in transport policy. Intense scrutiny, political debate and confrontation is forcing a shift away from traditional preoccupation with increasing transport supply, towards new and imaginative forms of demand management, diversification and 'transport efficiency'. In the UK, this conceptual transition is now firmly under way.

A comparison with the transition that began two decades ago in energy policy reveals important similarities and provides fresh analytic support for transport policy in three key areas: measuring changes in overall transport activity; improving overall national 'transport efficiency'; and exploring the possibilities of alternative, perhaps radically different, transport futures.

Individual statistics for vehicle, freight and people movements all tell only part of a bigger story. But different forms of transport benefit the same population, often share the same networks, take up a fraction of the same land area, lubricate the same economy, pollute the same biosphere and rely on the same overall stocks and sources of energy to keep them going. Summing the mass movement of people, goods and their 'carriers' gives the best unified measure of overall transport activity, 'gross mass movement'. This presents some analogy with the concept of total primary energy consumption and shares the weaknesses and strengths of this and other such measures, which hide the richer details to fulfil the need for simple and aggregated quantitative information.

In 1992, UK gross mass movement was equivalent to each woman, man and child driving a fully loaded 38-tonne goods vehicle 1.4 km each day. Only 22% of this mass movement was the actual productive movement of people and goods, the remainder being the incidental mass movement of transport carriers themselves. While 'useful' movements of people and goods in the UK have risen in line with GDP, gross mass movement has been rising more quickly. The ratio of gross mass movement to GDP, 'gross transport intensity', increased 20% between 1970 and 1992. This decline in the productivity of mass movement is a matter of concern and its causes need to be better understood.

Pressures for greater environmental protection, improved economic competitiveness, and enhanced levels of social welfare, health and safety, underlie the need to improve overall national transport efficiency. The analytical tools and concepts developed in energy efficiency indicate that no single measure alone – technological, fiscal or regulatory – will overcome the many barriers to improving energy efficiency. Many other factors apart from cost have prevented the economic and technical potential for greater efficiency being realised including, time, effort, culture, information, habits and addiction. Information programmes, financial incentives and tougher regulations and standards could help realize more of the technical and behavioural potential to improve transport efficiency.

Limits on social, environmental and engineering adaptation to transport growth highlight the need for analytical approaches that can expand our understanding of alternative scenarios for transport futures. Official UK National Road Traffic Forecasts for the next 30 years depict declining gross transport intensity but still a doubling of gross mass movement.

Alternative scenarios suggest that, among other things, modal shifts and modal efficiency improvements could play key roles in accelerating the decline in gross transport intensity.

# Foreword

Transport is a central and complex sector that is the focus of growing controversy in many OECD countries. It is frequently identified as posing particular problems for energy and environmental policy, and in many of these countries it is also the largest and fastest-growing energy end-use sector.

It is for these reasons that the Energy and Environmental Programme decided to undertake a research study on transport. Dr Stephen Peake, having recently completed his doctoral thesis on transport trends and policies and the lessons which might be derived from the energy experience, was an ideal candidate to undertake such research, and he joined us in September 1993. His report *Transport in Transition* draws partly upon the ideas he developed in collaboration with his doctoral supervisor, Dr Chris Hope, at the Department of Engineering, Cambridge University.

Stephen has worked hard to develop the work as a report for a publication by the Energy and Environmental Programme. The study argues that transport is entering a turbulent phase with potentially radical changes, and explores some of the lessons which may be drawn from the rich and complex history of energy trends, analysis and policy itself. It is a challenging approach which should stimulate much fresh thinking about the analysis and implications of transport trends and policies.

*July 1994*
                                                   Dr Michael Grubb
                        Head, Energy and Environmental Programme

# Chapter 1

## Introduction

*It is proper to consider the similar ...*
*even in things far distant from each other.*
ARISTOTLE, *METAPHYSICS*

Transport is a messy problem – it allows some of the most enjoyable experiences life can offer, yet at the same time lies at the heart of many environmental and social concerns. This report explores the thesis that a fundamental transition in transport policies and trends is occurring due to intensified conflicts between transport, environmental and social goals, and examines how experiences from the history of energy – another strategic policy area bearing many structural similarities with transport – can be used to illuminate the current debate on transport projections and policy. The empirical data within the report concentrate on transport in the UK, and the present circumstances described may most strongly parallel those in other West European countries. But the essence of the report – that transport concepts, policies and trends are undergoing a transition in which much can be learned from the history of energy – is potentially of global applicability.

Transport is inextricably linked to our economic and social well being. Modern transport systems underpin everything from just-in-time production and distribution networks to the convenience of regular visits to friends and relatives, and are the key enabling factor of where people live, work and make their recreation, and where economic activity takes place.

As the demand for transport continues to rise throughout the world's economies, transport's role in society is coming under increasing scrutiny and transport policy is turning out to be highly contentious. Transport has long been trying to cope with the challenge of balancing economic and welfare needs with environmental and social objectives. Rising transport demands produce many significant environmental, health and social problems. Traffic growth causes worsening congestion, noise and various forms of atmospheric and water pollution, while developing the infrastructure of modern transport often involves the loss of land, local facilities and pedestrian and cyclist freedoms. Congestion inhibits economic competitiveness while accidents, air pollution and problems of social isolation cost society much, and are growing.

The costs which greater mobility imposes conflict with the benefits it provides. This is leading to intense scrutiny, political debate and confrontation over the trends and future prospects for transport. Plans for further roads, airports and high-speed rail links are met with vociferous and increasingly effective opposition, introducing clear tensions between social, environmental and economic policy objectives. European governments espouse sustainable development and consider proposals to reduce traffic growth, while jobs, competitiveness and regional integration have been linked to the largest road improvement and construction programme ever in the UK and plans for expanded trans-European transport networks.

On the one side, the transition is being pushed by unprecedented concern over the conflicts between transport, the environment and economic competitiveness, while on the other, the transition is being encouraged by demands for increased standards of living and welfare. After a period of unprecedented growth in transport, a reconciliation would now appear to serve both sides of the conflict well. Implementing the spirit of sustainable mobility will involve the realignment of these pressures so that they begin to act constructively, in the same direction.

## 1.1 Energy in transition

The quadrupling of oil prices in the winter of 1973–74 produced deep shock waves within the energy sector and had a considerable psychological impact on the energy policy community. In the UK, it boosted efforts to develop fossil fuel resources – oil and gas from the North Sea, and coal – and prompted a set of proposals for an expanded nuclear power programme. It also sparked fundamental change in the evaluation of energy policies and strategies as well as a conceptual revolution in awareness and perception of energy use within society. The conceptual revolution had ramifications for the debate over energy futures. Our theoretical understanding of energy in society is now as advanced as that of any other resource management issue and contains, by any standards, some important ideas and elegant concepts.

Two decades on, the history of energy contains at least three developments which add fresh insights to the transition in transport:

- *Component demand and aggregate analysis*: common units of energy have been used to integrate different systems of measurement of the diverse forms in which energy occurs; and the development of rationalized systems of accounting have made better use of available information on energy demands and uses, and have provided an overview of the entire energy picture.
- *Demand management*: this was introduced as basic exhortations from government for people to use less energy but subsequently became a much richer variety of measures for increasing energy efficiency. Many practical measures have been explored to avoid inefficiency and encourage energy users to get more out of the use of less energy.
- *Futures analysis*: large, often unexpected discontinuities in the growth and use of energy in the economy have been observed; alternative ways of coping with uncertainty in energy planning were developed. Efforts shifted away from trying to predict the most likely future – traditionally the role of energy forecasting – towards attempts to develop alternative energy strategies, using scenario analysis within the planning process.

The analysis of complex issues within energy policy, such as the introduction of new energy technologies and the human, organizational and technical implications of growing energy demand, are treated as part of a much broader 'top-down' (see section 3.5) picture of change in the interaction between overall economic activity and the total aggregate demand for energy. Another influential development was the extension of the measurement of thermodynamic end-use efficiency to the broad level of economic systems as a whole: the introduction of the 'useful energy' demand concept prompted the question 'how much energy do we really need?' The answer formed the theoretical basis behind many of the energy conservation and efficiency programmes. The concepts of demand management and energy efficiency filtered into energy policy in the aftermath of the ,1973 oil crisis and with mixed success – two decades on, there is still room for further significant national energy efficiency improvements.

At the beginning of the 1970s most analysts and governments assumed that the demand for energy was hard-wired to economic growth and that therefore energy policy was a matter of ensuring adequate volume of supply and managing structural change. However, the 'rapids' of uncertainty which characterized the background to energy policy during the early 1970s led to the breakdown of some cherished energy-economic 'laws'. In light of the unexpected discontinuities in energy trends, scenario processes using a combination of top-down and bottom-up analysis proved much better able to explore emerging questions about energy needs.

## 1.2 Transport in transition → Road

The defeat of distance has long been a prerequisite of capitalism.[1] Initially, with the establishment of the railways, for example, travellers could only overcome the 'friction of space' through unparalleled industrial organization and social co-operation and even then access to the sparse technology was limited and expensive.[2] Now, even for the individual, distance is no longer a challenge. However, a new set of challenges has arisen. Roads are becoming saturated and distance has started to fight back. The challenge now is about coping with transport's impacts.

A fundamental transition in UK transport is emerging. There is a move away from preoccupation with expanding transport supply towards diversification, demand management and greater efficiency – similar in many respects to the energy transition of the 1970s. Limitations of infrastructure capacity are already forcing the allocation of different types of transport demands among the limited spaces and times available – peak spreading. At the micro level, the spreading of peak traffic over time and space is continuing

---

[1] F. Braudel, *Civilisation and Capitalism, 15–18 Century: Volume I, The Structures of Everyday Life*, Fontana, London, 1985.

[2] Å.E. Anderson, 'Infrastructure and the Transformation to the C-Society', in R. Thord (ed.), *The Future of Transportation and Communication*, Springer Verlag, Berlin, 1993, pp. 11–26.

to develop, while distinctions between different components of the demand for transport are sharpening – by journey purpose and by strategic importance. At the macro level, aggregated analyses of the broad relationship between overall patterns of transport and economic activity will have to be taken into account, in the same way that energy analysis sought to unify changes in the demand for particular fuels or technologies and relate them to broader macroscopic criteria. In transport, this means developing new ways of measuring all kinds of physical transport movements, whether they are of people, goods, services or the technologies which carry them. In particular, there seems great potential in a rationale which makes clear distinctions between 'useful' physical mass movements – essential movements of passengers or goods – and the physical mass movement of transport carriers themselves (often partly or wholly empty).

The traditional preoccupation with the supply side of transport policy – the provision of additional road, air and rail infrastructure to accommodate unconstrained transport growth – is no longer appropriate socially, economically and environmentally. In addition to using technology to treat the symptoms of transport growth – congestion, accidents, air pollution and social isolation – policy will have to begin to address the underlying causes of transport growth. Managing demand is an important part of the next stage for transport policy in the UK and elsewhere, and ideas on what forms analysis and policy should take are themselves in strong demand. The demand for transport is as heterogeneous as the landscape which moulds it and will not react obediently to naive and extreme calls for doing without. But as energy efficiency programmes have shown, over a sufficient period, there is a role for the sensible and considered co-ordination of several measures to help reduce the economy's vulnerable dependence on energy sources: the experience may reveal much about equivalent policies to reduce transport dependency through 'transport efficiency'.

Uncertainty surrounding social and environmental adaptation, and engineering limits to transport growth, highlight the need for analytical approaches that can expand our understanding of possible alternative transport futures – perhaps unexpected ones – including those in which policies either external or internal to the transport sector radically alter.

Calls for 'sustainable mobility' raise the prospects of ultimate limits on transport growth and challenge the traditional supply approach to transport forecasting and planning. The 'predict and provide' planning phenomenon is crumbling under growing uncertainty about new types of government and societal responses to current and possible future transport policies. The wider use of scenario analysis, refined in the context of energy planning in the 1970s and 1980s, offers a way of contemplating a broader range of alternative futures and coping with such uncertainty.

## 1.3 Aims and structure of the report

There is an acute need for constructive thinking about the pressures, prospects and possible responses to transport growth. Looking into the energy sector to see what has been happening there is one way of meeting part of this need. But drawing parallels between energy and transport is a challenging and subjective process. Before lessons can be drawn, connections have to be made. This requires a different way of looking at transport, in a way compatible with the ideas and concepts of energy. In comparing what amount to broad qualitative patterns of change in two different areas of public policy – energy and transport – the concepts covered and ideas generated within this report span a large area of 'policy space'. The use of the energy-transport analogy is intended to help look at an old problem in a new way and is not intended to generate a direct recipe for success.[3] This report aims to contribute to the learning process. The three themes which are taken up demonstrate how useful comparisons between the sectors may be made. It may be that the report stimulates comparisons between other aspects of the energy-transport analogy which are not covered. This is the intention – as with all good analogies, the ideas which they generate can sometimes have a life of their own.[4]

The energy sector is no stranger to 'black hat' thinking. There is no shortage of criticism of energy policy. Indeed many commentators have made it their business to show how bad in places it has been. Understanding why energy policies have not been as effective as they ought to, or could have been, is not

---

[3] It is important to stress that the report does not aim to focus on energy use within the transport sector. Instead, it aims to look at transport, but with the ideas of energy and energy policy in mind.

[4] E. de Bono, *Lateral Thinking*, Penguin, Harmondsworth, 1970.

the present aim. This report is about a lateral, constructive view of positive developments in energy for the benefit of transport thinking.

Taking the UK as an example, the trends, prospects and problems in the growth of transport are summarized in Chapter 2. The third chapter looks at the background to energy policy in the early 1970s, and summarizes developments in three areas which emerged from the transition towards greater diversification and demand management and efficiency. Chapter 4 then explores some of the limitations and strengths of the energy-transport analogy by analysing a range of both policy and structural differences and similarities. The remaining three chapters concentrate on three specific themes where transport can learn from energy. Chapter 5 develops a new way of measuring the overall aggregate relationship between transport and economic activity and applies this to UK historical data, to reveal trends for the period 1952–92. Chapter 6 explores parallels between energy and transport from the policy perspective, focusing on how energy efficiency offers new insight to the concept of 'transport efficiency'. The final chapter draws on the energy experience of using scenario analysis to explore uncertain futures, contrasting two radically alternative scenarios for the development of transport in the UK up to 2025.

# Chapter 2

## Transport Trends, Problems and Prospects: the Case of the UK

The way the world looks and feels today is strongly affected by developments in transport infrastructure and technology. The construction of dense networks of transport infrastructure – canals, railways, roads and airways – has played a central role in shaping economic transitions and looks set to continue to do so. Historically, a fundamental relationship between transport and the economy has been observed world-wide. As economies grow, so does the demand for transport. Initially this is largely related to trading patterns, then, as industrialization takes place, passenger transport grows rapidly as well.

As society becomes more mobile, significant changes occur in living and working patterns. Cheaper and faster transport allows greater specialization of economic production and allows residential populations to spread.[5] As populations begin to disperse, economic markets spread and the demands and expectations for personal mobility rise. The subsequent growth and evolution of transport under advanced and post-industrial conditions is a complex one. The possibility of transport becomes the opportunity and the opportunity becomes the expectation. The role of transport shifts from being purely a means – a process which enables social and economic activity to take place – towards partly being an end in itself. Over time, the production and maintenance of transport infrastructure itself becomes a large proportion of the economic activity which takes place alongside the increased demand for the manufacture of vehicles, their servicing and the production of the infrastructure to support them. In 1992, transport accounted, on average, for 15% of total household expenditure in the UK. More than two-thirds of households had at least one car and at least 1.5 million people (7% of the workforce) were employed directly in transport-related activities while transport provided 22% of total

---

[5] On the nature of the transition from the 'traditional' society to the 'advanced' society see J. Adams, *Transport Planning: Vision and Practice*, Routledge and Kegan Paul, London, 1981. For an example of more recent changes in urban land use patterns see J. Garreau, *Edge City: Life on the New Frontier*, Doubleday, New York, 1991. The relocation of business activity towards the outskirts of US urban centres is a stark indication of this process.

government customs and excise taxation.[6] Habit and incomes continue to create still further demand for personal mobility and goods transport.

To industry and commerce, transport has always been an important factor of production, while, for a significant and growing proportion of the world's population, transport has a profound and complex effect on the structure of daily life. Competitiveness in the market place or full participation in society begins to rely more and more on access to the expanding transport networks. In the UK in 1991, people spent, on average, about an hour per day moving around.[7]

In turn, the growing demand for personal mobility and freight movement is now linked with some of the most important social and environmental problems of our time. On the global scale, potential climate instability, local air pollution and resource depletion are accounted for in no small measure by the global economy's seemingly limitless desire for increased motorized mobility and accommodation of global trade. At the local level, the deleterious side-effects of the use and abuse of transport infrastructures are all too obvious. Street life retreats behind closed doors, social problems continue, the health of those who have to live by busy roads suffers and auto-related crime rises. These problems, once just side-effects, are becoming increasingly central to transport policy which is now beginning to focus as much on coping as it does on 'getting there'.

If not for any other reason, then the mounting social and environmental problems of transport – which successive generations of technology and policies have failed to solve – are themselves likely to catalyse a historic shift in the relationship between transport and economic growth.

## 2.1 The growth of transport in the UK: structure and influences

The demand for passenger and freight transport has exploded over the last few decades throughout the developed world, and most of this by road. There are, however, significant differences in the relationships between transport activity, population and economic activity throughout different areas of the

---

[6] Department of Transport, *Transport Statistics Great Britain, 1993*, HMSO, London, 1993. Central Statistical Office, *National Accounts 1993*, HMSO, London, 1993.

[7] Department of Transport, *National Travel Survey 1989/91*, HMSO, London, 1993. In the UK in 1991, the average speed for all journeys (over 50 metres) and modes was 29 km per hour. The average distance travelled per person per year over all journeys and all modes was 10,368 km. On average, the total time spent travelling was 370 hours per year – or 1 hour per person per day.

world including within Europe (Figure 2.1). Compared with the European average, the UK has slightly higher levels of car ownership, and passenger and freight transport. The comparable figures for Japan and the US show that while Japan is close to the European pattern, the US pattern is much more intensive. International comparisons show that gross domestic product (GDP) is a main determinant of passenger and freight transport, but also that many other factors including pricing regimes, regulatory styles, historic/ cultural influences and the availability and quality of public transit systems are important and, in particular, can reduce car ownership and use.[8]

The structure and main influences underlying transport growth can again be illustrated with respect to the UK. Figure 2.2A illustrates how the growth in passenger transport demand in the forty years from 1952 to 1992 rested entirely upon growth in personal road use; total passenger kilometres trebled in a UK population which grew by only 15% – a rise in average yearly travel per person from 4,500 km in 1952 to 12,200 km in 1992. This comprised expansion of car ownership from 14% of all households in 1951 to 68% in 1991 – a third of which now have more than one car – coupled with a 20% increase in average annual distance driven per car.[9]

Analysis of travel purpose shows that since 1965, personal travel increased across all three main types of journey (Figure 2.2B), but with increases in 'personal business' (i.e. shopping and access to other services) and leisure travel (i.e. social, entertainment and holidays) accounting for more than two-thirds of the total increase.[10] Travel, in other words, is increasingly for personal and 'discretionary' purposes.[11] The 50% increase in distance travelled for

---

[8] On the international comparisons of trends in passenger travel between these regions see e.g. J. Kenworthy and P. Newman, *Automobile Dependence – "The Irresistible Force"?*, University of Technology, Sydney, 1993. On contrasting styles of environmental regulation in transport see M.P. Walsh, 'Environmental Regulation of Transport: US, OECD and Global Trends in Legislation and Policy', in T. Sterner (ed.), *Economic Policies for Sustainable Development*, Kluwer, Amsterdam, 1994, pp. 240–260.

[9] Department of Transport, *Transport Statistics Great Britain, 1993*.

[10] Figures are for journeys over 1 mile which in 1991 accounted for 42% of all journeys but just 2% of all distance travelled.

[11] See e.g. S. Town, 'Transport and Social Structure: Some British Evidence', in *Social Aspects of Transport: How To Use Social Research in Transport Policy Making*, Supplementary Report Number 689, Transport and Road Research Laboratory, Crowthorne, 1982, pp. 115–131. The distinction between fixed (e.g. work and education), variable and discretionary travel is a useful device from a policy perspective as it suggests there may be greater possibility of changing travel patterns for one particular type of journey above another.

*Transport trends, problems and prospects:*

**Figure 2.1 European, US and Japanese levels of car ownership, passenger transport per capita and freight transport per unit GDP, 1991**[12]

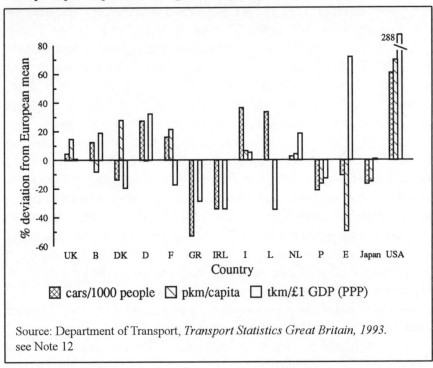

Source: Department of Transport, *Transport Statistics Great Britain, 1993*.
see Note 12

work and education was due to an increase in the average length of these journeys by 81%, offsetting a 17% reduction in the average number of these journeys per week.

Wealth is the dominant factor increasing travel consumption, though a variety of other socio-economic factors also play a role such as: demographic shifts towards middle and old age groups and increases in rural populations – who tend to rely more on cars than public transport compared with other social groups; the changing social role of women, more of whom have entered employment and taken up driving; and the nature of specialized work –

[12] See footnotes 13 and 16 for definition of pkm and tkm. Data for pkm/capita for GR, IRL and L are not included in the figure. Also note that US data on tkm/£1 GDP (purchasing power parity) have been 'capped' in the figure since they are 288% above the European mean and this makes it difficult to see variations between other variables in a figure of this form.

**Figure 2.2 Overall UK passenger transport, by mode (A) and journey purpose (B): 1952–1992**[13]

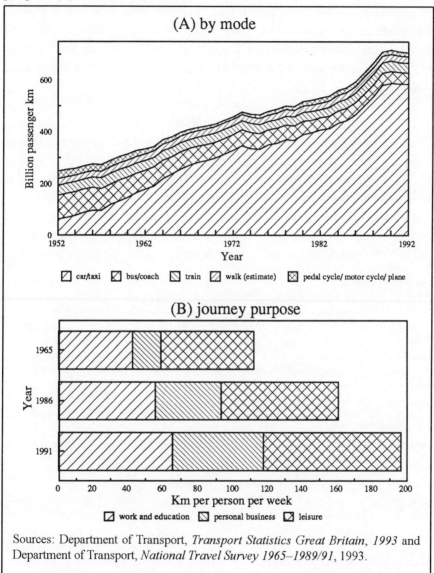

Sources: Department of Transport, *Transport Statistics Great Britain, 1993* and Department of Transport, *National Travel Survey 1965–1989/91*, 1993.

---

[13] Passenger transport is conventionally measured in terms of passenger kilometres (pkm – sometimes stated as billion pkm or bpkm) with one passenger kilometre equivalent to one passenger travelling one kilometre (drivers of cars are included as passengers, but drivers of buses, goods vehicles, trains or planes are not).

demanding an increasingly mobile workforce, willing to travel further.[14]

Figure 2.3A shows corresponding trends in freight transport. Total goods movements in the UK more than doubled between 1952 and 1992; and again this is due almost entirely to increases in road haulage.[15] Detailed analysis of the level and composition of road freight from 1962 to 1992 shows that there was roughly a doubling across all categories of goods transported by road (Figure 2.3B).[16]

The growth in road freight has been closely coupled to GDP.[17] In detail, however, there have been many different influences upon the growth: decisions about where to locate plant and distribution facilities taken partly in response to access to labour; regional planning policy; and the continued development of new manufacturing techniques and service industries including 'just-in-time' delivery, promoting more frequent and smaller batch distribution.

In summary, economic growth in the UK in recent decades stimulated rapid growth in road transport, both directly through increased freight movements and also through rising household incomes which support wider car ownership,

---

[14] In 1991, people in the UK without cars travelled on average 90 km per week while people in households with one car travelled 210 km per week and people in those households with two cars 315 km per week; while 95% of households in the top fifth income group had a car, 30% of households in the bottom fifth income group had a car: Department of Transport, *National Travel Survey 1989/91*, 1993 and Central Statistical Office, *Family Spending: A report on the 1992 Family Spending Survey*, HMSO, London 1993. See also P.B. Goodwin, 'Demographic Impacts, Social Consequences, and the Transport Policy Debate', *Oxford Review of Economic Policy*, Vol.6, No.2, 1990, pp.76–90. In 1991 women still travelled significantly less distance per week than men – 215 km for women compared with 335 km for men – although the gap is shrinking as more of the female population take up driving. Whereas in 1975, 70% of men were qualified to drive and only 29% of women, by 1992 the gap between men and women had shrunk significantly with 80% of men and 69% of women being qualified to drive.

[15] There has been a marked decline in rail freight. The statistics show a substantial increase in domestic waterborne freight (mostly the coastal bulk movements of oil and gas from the North Sea) in 1976, but this was due to a change in the statistical definitions employed.

[16] Department of Transport, *Transport Statistics Great Britain, 1964–1974*, HMSO, London, 1975; Department of Transport, *Transport Statistics Great Britain, 1993*. Freight activity is conventionally measured in units of tonne kilometres (tkm or billion tkm – btkm), with one tonne kilometre equivalent to one tonne of goods moving a distance of one kilometre.

[17] For a detailed analysis of historical trends in freight transport income elasticity see A.S. Fowkes, C.A. Nash, J.P. Toner and G. Tweddle, *Disaggregated Approaches to Freight Analysis: A Feasibility Study*, ITS Working Paper 399, Institute for Transport Studies, University of Leeds, Leeds, 1993.

**Figure 2.3 UK freight transport 1952–92, by mode indexed with GDP (A) and composition (B)**

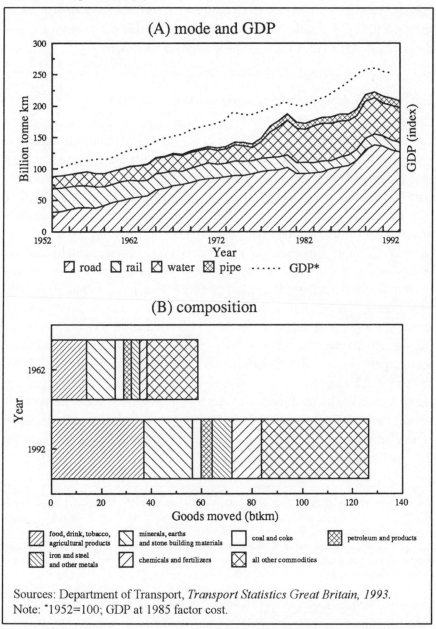

Sources: Department of Transport, *Transport Statistics Great Britain, 1993.*
Note: *1952=100; GDP at 1985 factor cost.

in turn promoting more frequent and longer personal journeys, particularly discretionary. The construction, production and maintenance of the road transport infrastructures and the vehicles which use them have, in turn, supported economic growth and enabled such valued personal mobility. However, there are now considerable doubts over the sustainability of such trends.


## 2.2 The environmental and social impacts of transport

Growing passenger and freight transport is as good a measure as any of the many benefits which the movement of people and goods brings to economic and social life: they are also a good indicator of the problems which transport activity brings. Indeed, it is hard to dissociate the benefits from the problems transport has brought to society – the two are inextricably linked. The potential of transport to fulfil travel aspirations and enable greater choice of where people live, work and spend free time is being offset by its contribution to some of the most important economic, social and environmental problems which society faces.[18] Unlike some public policy problems perhaps, for the person on the street the transport problem is real and tangible: a large proportion of the population spends on average more than an hour each day seeing, feeling and smelling it. As congestion spills over to more roads and throughout the day, for most of the population getting about is becoming increasingly dissatisfying. Attitudes are changing in the freight sector too. Industry's tolerance for 'wild roadways, free spirits and general unpredictability' appears to be finally wearing thin.[19] Instead there are calls for controls which enable more predictability and fewer surprises. Much greater attention is now being focused on the problems of transport, particularly traffic growth. Marcia Lowe summarizes this position:

---

[18] On the distinction between 'need' and 'aspiration' in terms of the demand for transport see H.T. Dimitriou, *Urban Transport Planning: A Developmental Perspective*, Routledge, London, 1992. The only real travel needs are those of 'survival', the rest are the fulfilment of certain aspirations – the attractiveness of which falls as the full social cost of fulfilling them increases. Transport policies which shift patterns of transport towards sustainable mobility will find it difficult not to establish a position which recognizes and exploits this distinction.

[19] R.J. Schonberger, 'Taming the Wild Roadways: Teamwork, Communication, and Synchronization Across Space', in Thord, *The Future of Transportation and Communication*, p. 85.

The automobile once promised a dazzling world of speed, freedom, and convenience, magically conveying people where the road would take them. Given these alluring qualities, it is not surprising that people around the world enthusiastically embraced the dream of car ownership. But societies that have built their transport systems around the automobile are now waking up to a much harsher reality. The problems created by over reliance on the car are outweighing its benefits.[20]

Such views are now common in the community of independent transport researchers, and increasingly reflected in popular opinion.[21] The vehicle – the icon of mass society – has become the victim of its own success. In 1992, the European Commission found that over half (54%) of those people questioned in Europe had 'very much or quite a lot of reason' to complain about the problems that traffic caused to their local environment.[22] It is likely that public frustration and irritation will play an increasingly important role in bringing about greater political awareness and responsiveness.

Since road transport is dominant, it is also the culprit of many of these impacts – although all forms of motorized transport have their own social and environmental problems. Transport has a range of impacts on the environment and society which can be quantified and which transport policies are increasingly being urged to address. In addition to the familiar, but still growing, problems of congestion, noise and land-take, the impact of transport on air quality is considerable and perceptions of this are growing (Figure 2.4).

Recently much effort has been put into assigning monetary values to transport problems – although the monetary figures often provoke controversy (Box 2.1).

---

[20] M.D. Lowe, *Alternatives to the Automobile: Transport for Liveable Cities*, Worldwatch Paper No. 98, Worldwatch Institute, Washington, 1990.

[21] See e.g. S. Nadir and J.J. Mackenzie, *Car Trouble*, World Resources Institute, Boston, 1993; W. Zuckerman, *The End of the Road*, The Lutterworth Press, Cambridge, 1991; D. Engwicht, *Towards an Eco-City: Calming the Traffic*, Envirobook, Sydney, 1993; European Commission, *Europeans and the Environment in 1992*, Eurobarometer 37.0, European Commission, Brussels, 1992.

[22] European Commission, *Europeans and the Environment in 1992*.

**Figure 2.4 Air quality: the records of the UK transport sector**

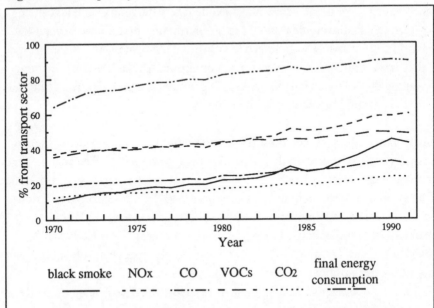

black smoke    NOx    CO    VOCs    CO₂    final energy consumption

Source: Department of Environment, *Digest of Environmental Protection and Water Statistics,* HMSO, London, 1992.

Some problems, for example congestion and accidents, are endemic to the nature of transport itself and therefore are not new, while technology has relegated others to the status of merely transitory. As Foley writes:

A Victorian, seeing the growth of horse-drawn traffic, might have extrapolated a graph of manure deposition in the streets of London and concluded the city would be submerged by now.[23]

Several transport problems have come and gone like this – for example, pothole drownings (1700s), horse manure (1800s), road dust (1900s) and lead pollution (1970s). But with the exceptions of the departure of medium-term energy security concerns and the arrival of the greenhouse gas problem, a list of today's concerns over the problems of transport activity, primarily 'external costs' as they are now regularly portrayed in the language of economics, is no different

[23] G. Foley, *The Energy Question*, Penguin, Harmondsworth, 1981.

**Box 2.1 Quantifiable transport problems: some monetary estimates for the UK**

## ROAD

*Accidents*

In 1992, 4,229 people were killed, and 310,673 suffered some kind of injury on Britain's roads.* Using official monetary estimates of the values of a statistical life and of the costs of injuries, total monetary costs of accidents in the UK in 1992 amounted to £9,900 million. It could be argued that some of the costs of injuries to motorists are in fact internalized through their own risk perception. However, this is perhaps offset by the exclusion of other costs in this calculation, such as the anxiety and fear that children, parents and older people, suffer with regard to road traffic. An overall figure greater than £10,000 million would not seem unreasonable.

*Congestion*

Current congestion costs in the UK have been estimated to be at least £13,000 million, though their level is a contentious issue.**

## ALL MODES

*Air pollution* (see Figure 2.4)

Altogether, the total cost of air pollution in the UK in 1992 (excluding volatile organic compounds) can be estimated at over £3,000 million – over £2,000 million of which is due to emissions of particulates.[†]

*Noise*

In 1991, road traffic accounted for 63% of all noise sources outside dwellings in the UK. The monetary value of noise cost in the UK is estimated at around 0.1% of GDP or £600 million – very small compared with other external problems.[‡]

The total cost of these impacts comes to £27,000 million or around 5% of GDP - though there are enormous uncertainties in this figure.

* Department of Transport, *Transport Statistics Great Britain, 1993*.
** D. Pearce, *Blueprint 3: Measuring Sustainable Development*, Earthscan, London, 1994. Contention arises over the extent to which congestion is endemic to urban living – see M.J.H. Mogridge, *Travel in Towns*, Macmillan, London, 1990.
[†] Department of Environment, *Digest of Environmental Protection and Water Statistics*, HMSO, London, 1992. Values per tonne of emissions taken from Pearce, *Blueprint 3*, (table 10.4).
[‡] Ibid.

in its basic content from those which were being drawn up in the early 1970s.[24]

Some problems have been alleviated. Road deaths in the UK, for example, are down to their lowest level since records began in 1926.[25] Others problems, however, have got worse. Congestion, for example, is getting more acute and more widespread, while the transport sector's contribution to total energy consumption and emissions has been rising (Figure 2.4).[26]

Transport in the UK has several unwanted environmental distinctions. It is:

- the largest and fastest-growing end-use energy sector;
- the largest and fastest-growing emitter of particulates (black smoke);
- responsible for 90% of carbon monoxide (CO) emissions;
- the largest and fastest-growing emitter of nitrogen oxides (NOx).

Against the background of an unprecedented increase in general environmental consciousness, concerns over the external costs of transport are now receiving a higher profile than ever before.[27] Given 150 years of improvements in economic productivity and technical efficiency, Foley's Victorian might well ask why these forces have not yet been successfully applied to the negative impacts of transport activity.

*Unintended social effects*
Transport is also responsible for a range of unintended social impacts. Unlike air pollution and accidents, for example, other social effects cannot readily be measured or valued but are nevertheless real and important. Once again, since road transport is dominant, it is also responsible for many of these unintentional social effects, although disturbance from aircraft and trains can also be important

---

[24] For example, compare K. Button, *Transport Economics*, Edward Elgar, Aldershot, 1993, with Independent Commission on Transport, *Changing Directions*, Coronet, London, 1973.
[25] See Box 2.1. On average, 11 people per day die on the UK's roads.
[26] Department of Transport, *Transport Statistics Great Britain, 1993*. Statistics show that average speeds through the day in central, inner and outer London areas are all, albeit very slowly, decreasing.
[27] See e.g. J. Whitelegg, *Transport for a Sustainable Future*, Belhaven, London, 1993, and OECD, *Market and Government Failures in Environmental Management: The Case of Transport*, OECD, Paris, 1992.

to those who live or work close by. A root cause of many of these effects stems from the space which road traffic typically consumes – space that could otherwise be used for other social interaction.[28] The inhospitability of streets due to the danger, noise and smell of road traffic prevents valuable social interactions taking place. The result is that road traffic diminishes the health and quality of life for those who live by it and is increasingly forcing people to make considerable social and behavioural adaptations.[29]

The redistribution of homes, schools, public facilities, leisure activities and work places around access to the motor car has been a defining characteristic of the twentieth century.[30] There is now intensified interest as to whether or not the sum of the benefits to individuals derived from high levels of motorized transport is greater than the costs to society as a whole. Increasing car use and dependency for the majority impose significant costs on the minority who cannot, or do not, wish to use cars (32% of households in GB in 1992). These people have to suffer the costs of others' car use without gaining any of the benefits – and often, as a result, have to pay higher prices for lower-quality public transport services. People on low incomes spend less on travel and travel less; in other words, relative to those on higher incomes they adapt by reducing their consumption – and hence social participation – rather than reduce spending on other essential goods and services.[31]

The inequalities between those people who have access to cars and those who do not represents social inequity in transport. There is some analogy here with the poor often spending a greater proportion of their incomes on heating and fuel.[32] Unlike fuel poverty, transport poverty results in a loss of

---

[28] I. Illich, *Energy and Equity*, Calder and Boyars, London, 1974. Illich writes 'Beyond a critical speed, no one can save time without forcing others to lose it' (p. 42).
[29] Engwicht, *Towards an Eco-City: Calming the Traffic*. Adaptations such as significant increases in the escorting of children to and from school in the UK – see M. Hillman, J. Adams and J. Whitelegg, *One False Move: A Study of Children's Independent Mobility*, Policy Studies Institute, London, 1991.
[30] See Royal Town Planning Institute, *Traffic Growth and Planning Policy*, London Research Centre, London, 1991.
[31] On social goods and participation see A. Dilnot and D. Helm, 'Energy Policy, Merit Goods and Social Security', *Fiscal Studies*, Vol. 8, No. 3, 1987, pp. 29–45.
[32] On fuel poverty see B. Boardman, *Fuel Poverty: From Cold Homes to Affordable Warmth*, Belhaven, London, 1991.

participation in society – in the form of less travel – rather than a loss of disposable income.[33]

Other important negative social effects related to road transport activity include: increased alienation from other people as personal interaction between motorists is limited; increased domestic isolation caused by parked cars and the reduction in the number of facilities accessible on foot; parental fear of road accidents; personal security implications for those who have no access to cars (because of cars, there are fewer people walking and using public transport, so it becomes more dangerous for the few, especially in the hours of darkness)[34]; and community division and disturbance. While many of these factors cannot be quantified, the impact of car ownership on crime can. In 1992, vehicle crime accounted for 28% of all reported crime in England and Wales.[35]

Just how much more traffic can be accommodated before the benefits of greater mobility really cease to outweigh these negative impacts is now a matter for urgent debate.

## 2.3 Transport in transition?

Two parallel strategies are emerging in response to the problems of transport growth. The first treats the underlying causes of transport growth and the second treats its symptoms – prevention and cure. Technology promises to cure some of the symptoms. The commercial development of cleaner, vastly more efficient, perhaps non-fossil-fuelled 'supervehicles' is very likely within the next decade. These will help to reduce some of the negative impacts of motorized transport – energy consumption, atmospheric emissions (including

---

[33] Central Statistical Office, *Family Spending: A Report on the 1992 Family Spending Survey*. In households in the lowest income quintile, weekly expenditure on transport was £6.98 out of a total weekly income of £94.22 (7%), whereas households in the highest quintile spent £92.72 out of a total income of £516.28 (18%). Data from the 1991 National Travel Survey shows that the average distance travelled per person per week (all modes) in the lowest 'real household income equivalent' quintile was a quarter of that per person in the highest income quintile – 92 vs 354 km per person per week.

[34] S.T. Aitkins, 'Personal Security as a Transport Issue: A State of the Art Review', *Transport Reviews*, Vol. 10, No. 2, 1990, pp. 111–125.

[35] Home Office, *Criminal Statistics England and Wales*, Cm 2410, HMSO, London, 1992–93.

perhaps $CO_2$ – although this depends on the fuel sources used), and perhaps some of the noise problem. However, the penetration of such technologies will take some time and even then will not reduce all the environmental and social impacts associated with road vehicles. In road systems that are at, or near, saturation for parts of the day already, even small increases in traffic result in dramatic swings from the benefits of such increases towards the costs they generate. Problems such as congestion, land-take, accidents, community severance, noise and visual intrusion will still remain. For the balance between the benefits and the costs of transport to be maintained, strategic policy responses as well as technology will be needed. Demand management could help to resolve some of the remaining conflicts between transport growth and environmental and social goals. Managing transport demand has already become a significant part of policy in parts of the US, some European countries (the Netherlands in particular) and is now under discussion in a wider range of OECD countries.[36]

It is in the well-known physical nature of the flow of traffic on busy roads to enter phases of turbulence, unpredictability and rapid change – once a certain maximum flow capacity is reached, the addition of further traffic quickly turns free flow into a stop-start jam. The social and economic capacity of the transport system – the point at which the balance between the benefits which increased motorized mobility brings to individuals starts to be offset by the costs to society as a whole – is less well defined, but still critically important. Whatever the economic and social capacity of the transport system, any further increases in transport beyond this are likely to induce sudden, unpredictable and rapid attitude changes and policy responses towards transport. Just as there are a range of local factors determining the engineering capacity of a road, a number of policy, psychological and political factors determine the social and environmental capacity to accommodate further (real or projected)

---

[36] The Californian approach to transportation demand management is summarized in M. Wachs, 'Learning from Los Angeles: Transport, Urban Form, and Air Quality', *Transportation*, Vol. 20, 1993, pp. 329–354. The Netherlands approach is outlined in detail in Second Chamber of the States-General, 20 922 No. 16, *Second Transport Structure Plan*, Session 1989–1990. The background to the emergence of demand management in the UK is summarized in P.B. Goodwin, *The New Regional Transport Strategy for the South-East: Key Issues in Demand Management*, Paper 771, University of Oxford, Oxford, 1993.

traffic increases – the turning point of an important transition away from preoccupation with increasing transport supply and towards demand management, diversification and transport efficiency.

Transport in the UK reached this critical level somewhere shortly after the Department of Transport's 1989 National Road Traffic Forecasts (NRTF) which predicted roughly a doubling of road traffic in the UK by 2025 (Figure 2.5) and the largest ever UK road building programme. Goodwin synthesized a new philosophy characterizing the transition towards demand management which recognizes that it will not be possible to supply the extra road space to accommodate the forecast levels of extra traffic:

> Since the publication of the revised road traffic forecasts in May 1989, there is now a radically new situation. The new feature is that, for the first time, there is universal recognition that there is no possibility of increasing road supply at a level which approaches the forecast increases in traffic.[37]

Doubt about both urban and inter-urban road building as part of an overall strategic transport policy has begun to reach government. The original 1989 forecasts (the latest in an important series of forecasts used in the appraisal and planning of investment in national road transport infrastructure) and the road programme to go with them continue to have important political significance. The government has linked a review of the methodology underlying them to its strategy for sustainable development.[38]

The UK government has recently recognized the need for traffic restraint and the introduction of demand management, particularly in view of its policy for sustainable development:

> The Government recognises that forecast levels of traffic growth, especially in urban areas, cannot be met in full and that new road building or the upgrading of existing highways will in some cases be environmentally

---

[37] Goodwin, 'Demographic Impacts, Social Consequences, and the Transport Policy Debate', p. 87.
[38] Review of methodology announced in *Sustainable Development: The UK Strategy*, Cm 2426, HMSO, London, 1994.

## Figure 2.5 The UK official forecast of traffic, 1988–2025

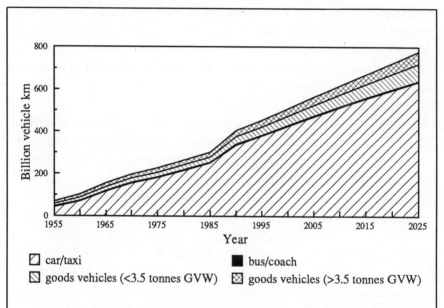

Year

☑ car/taxi ■ bus/coach
◫ goods vehicles (<3.5 tonnes GVW) ⊠ goods vehicles (>3.5 tonnes GVW)

Source: Department of Transport, *National Road Traffic Forecasts (Great Britain) 1989*, HMSO, London, 1989.
Note: The forecasts were in the form of a low and a high prediction. This represents the midpoint. The forecasts only predict traffic levels for cars, buses and goods vehicles.

unacceptable. It is Government policy not to build new trunk or local roads simply to facilitate commuting by car into the more congested urban centres.[39]

Transport is also increasingly seen as the weakest link in achieving a variety of policy goals in the energy and environmental sectors, and it is likely to continue to come under greater scrutiny from all sides. By 1993, a tangible shift in government policy towards transport was becoming evident with the publication of a report on planning measures to reduce $CO_2$ emissions, which

---

[39] Department of Environment and Department of Transport, *Planning Policy Guidance Note 13: Transport*, para 1.4, HMSO, London, 1994.

recommended diversification and further measures to manage demand.[40] The following year this was backed up by official guidance from the UK Departments of the Environment and Transport which emphasized, for the first time, a clear endorsement of the need for transport demand management.[41] The government has expressed clear concern about sustainable development and the environmental impacts of traffic growth.

It is not the Government's job to tell people where and how to travel. But if people continue to exercise their choices as they are at present and there are no other significant changes, the resulting traffic growth would have unacceptable consequences for both the environment and the economy of certain parts of the country, and could be very difficult to reconcile with overall sustainable development goals.[42]

However, whilst the broad notion of sustainability is well defined – meeting the needs of the present without compromising possibilities for the future – it is difficult to interpret the transport implications of sustainability when translated down from that broad level.[43]

Although evidence of this new policy style is now in many official policy documents, the reality has yet to hit government action. The recent reappraisal of the basis of the roads programme shows that the dominant policy approach is still unequivocally fixated on improving and increasing road supply. Although the fall-out from the 1989 forecasts has had a considerable impact on transport thinking outside government, it has yet to have a tangible impact

---

[40] Department of the Environment and Department of Transport, *Reducing Transport Emissions Through Planning*, HMSO, London, 1993.
[41] Department of Environment and Department of Transport, *Planning Policy Guidance Note 13: Transport.*
[42] *Sustainable Development: The UK Strategy*, p. 173.
[43] Commission of the European Communities, *The Impact of Transport on the Environment, Com (92) 46 final, Commission of the European Communities*, Brussels, 1992. This green paper on transport and the environment failed to interpret sustainable mobility successfully, either qualitatively or quantitatively. See also G. Stokes and J. Dargay, *What is a Sustainable Transport Policy? Research Paper 760*, Transport Studies Unit, University of Oxford, Oxford, 1993.

on the balance of government spending between roads and other alternatives.[44]

Transport policy in the UK is entering a new age of constraint – just as energy policy underwent its transformation as a result of the oil crisis in the early 1970s. Those familiar with developments in energy policy may recognize, at once, that the analogy suggests that this new phase may also become characterized as an age of innovation.

A transition in transport is occurring – deep pressures for growth are finally coming up against rising negative impacts, and even more rapidly rising perceptions of them – the exact timing of which remains uncertain, but which history might well date back to the NRTF reactions as the beginning of the watershed. The history of energy suggests that radical changes can occur on even the most apparently entrenched trends. It would be as well to study this history to learn what possible forms the transport transition may take.

---

[44] Department of Transport, *Trunk Roads in England 1994 Review*, HMSO, London, 1994. This recent 'recasting' of the roads programme knocked only 10% of the total value off £4,500,000 priority schemes now under consideration.

# Chapter 3

## Energy in Transition

The history of energy is the story of many transitions – transitions in the types of fuels used, in energy conversion devices and technologies, in institutional approaches towards the fuel and power industries and in the understanding of energy as a concept itself. From wood to fossil fuels then on to electricity, the profile of energy demand steadily changes in response to the development of new technologies and the discovery and harnessing of new energy sources. Although energy has been used in many of its multiple forms for several centuries, the scientific and policy understanding of energy has changed dramatically over the last two hundred years. Scientifically, energy has evolved from substance, to heat, to work and mathematical construct while energy policy analysis has dealt successively with individual fuels, their equivalent energy contents and the end-uses energy is needed for.

Two decades ago, the energy sector entered a period of intensified flux, including extensive change within energy policy analysis. Constraints on oil supply raised the prospect of energy demands having to be matched or, if necessary, limited to available supplies. Although the perception of an energy supply shortage has now disappeared it has had a lasting effect upon the normative philosophy behind energy policy.[45] The 1973 oil crisis catalysed an important reaction between two distinct approaches to energy policy analysis and planning. The traditional supply approach to energy policy – characterized by its emphasis on ensuring the availability of cheap and plentiful supplies of fuels to meet increasing energy demands – was supplemented with a new

---

[45] British Petroleum, *Statistical Review of World Energy, June 1993*, British Petroleum, London, 1993. Although the ratio of reserves to production – a measure of how long reserves would last if production continued at current levels – is greater than ever before at 43 (differing widely from region to region), for many nations energy security is still an important part of energy policy – see e.g. Commission of the European Communities, 'A View to the Future', *Energy in Europe* (special issue September 1992), Commission of the European Communities, Brussels, 1992.

demand-oriented approach. Two decades on, it is now chiefly environmental concerns which continue to push for more effective government actions to manage energy demand – changing the rules of the energy consumption game has been difficult and the process is still going on. This chapter summarizes the background to the energy transition and focuses on changes in three specific areas of energy policy analysis, planning and implementation which occurred as a result.

## 3.1 UK energy 1950–92

In the postwar period up to 1973, the energy profiles – the mix of different types of energy supply in the economy – of industrialized nations around the world were already changing rapidly. A major shift away from coal towards oil and petroleum products was underway and energy consumption was rising steadily with economic growth. Figure 3.1 shows the evolution of the primary energy mix in the UK up to and following 1973, and presents a typical picture of the sort of changes which were occurring prior to 1973 in different countries throughout the industrialized world.

In the immediate period after 1947, the UK economy was heavily dependent on coal (90% of primary energy consumption). Energy policy was coal policy.[46] This perception was, however, soon to evaporate with the rise of rapidly expanding domestic and international petroleum markets. Steady economic growth in the UK and other countries throughout most of the 1950s and 1960s was fuelled almost entirely by increases in oil consumption (coal consumption in the UK, for example, peaked in 1956) and energy policy was concerned primarily with ensuring the availability of enough energy supplies to meet rising demands. The discovery of natural gas at Groningen in the Netherlands in 1959 increased the likelihood of further substantial discoveries of oil and gas in the North Sea and marked the beginning of a new phase in the development of UK energy policy. The possibility of ample indigenous supplies of oil and gas created an optimistic view about energy supplies, characterized so well in the portrayal of the UK as an 'island of coal in a sea

---

[46] See D. Pearce, *UK Energy Policy: An Historical Overview*, Department of Political Economy, Discussion Paper 82-02, University of Aberdeen, Aberdeen, 1982.

## Figure 3.1 UK primary energy consumption by fuel: 1950–1992

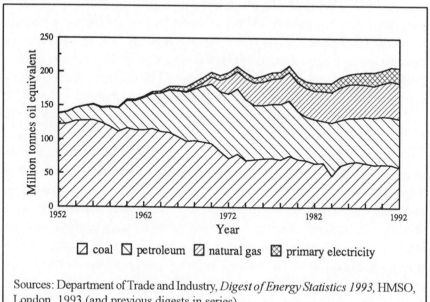

Year

☑ coal  ☒ petroleum  ⧄ natural gas  ⊠ primary electricity

Sources: Department of Trade and Industry, *Digest of Energy Statistics 1993*, HMSO, London, 1993 (and previous digests in series).

of oil and gas'.[47] There was also the prospect of cheap nuclear electricity.[48] The development of nuclear power and North Sea oil and gas marked the beginning of a more diverse approach to fuel and power policy.[49]

Meanwhile, environmental concerns had been rising steadily in the late 1960s and were an important feature of the early 1970s energy policy arena. In 1972, a working party known as the 'Club of Rome' published a much cited report concerning the 'limits to growth'.[50] The limits to growth debate typified the feeling of doom about the future which characterized the period.[51] This

---

[47] Ibid.
[48] P.L. Cook and A.J. Surrey, *Energy Policy*, Martin Robertson, London, 1977.
[49] HMSO, *Fuel Policy*, Cmnd 3438, HMSO, London, 1967. R. Bending and R. Eden, *UK Energy: Structures, Prospects and Policies*, Cambridge University Press, Cambridge, 1984. Energy policy was essentially managed by a consensus that increased energy demands had to be met by intensifying energy production and diversifying the economy's fuel mix.
[50] D.H. Meadows, D.L. Meadows, J. Randers and W.W. Behrens III, *The Limits to Growth*, Earth Island, London, 1972.
[51] See J. Gershuny, 'Are We Running Out of Time?', *Futures*, Vol. 24, No. 3, 1992, pp. 3–19.

pessimism was about to be further exacerbated by political events in the Middle East. On 6 October 1973, Egypt and Syria invaded Israeli-occupied territory, two days before a meeting of the Organization of Petroleum Exporting Countries (OPEC) in Vienna. Within two weeks, OPEC announced unilateral price increases and production cuts and an embargo on the shipment of oil to the United States and the Netherlands. The 1973 oil crisis had begun, and the chronic 'energy problem' emerged. Oil prices rose rapidly from around $3 to $12 a barrel, and revealed the growing vulnerability of most industrial economies to changes in the oil price and to supply disruption.

It was not, however, just fears over the security of oil supply that created a sense of an 'energy problem'; there were at least three more factors which defined its boundary conditions: first, it was not clear at all just how much oil and gas the world had in reserve; second, there was a great deal of uncertainty about future demand for energy; and third, environmental concerns over the impacts of energy production and use which had emerged in the early 1970s were being consolidated. The selective cuts in oil production imposed by OPEC had severe repercussions throughout the world and over a long period of time. In the UK, primary energy consumption in 1977 was lower than in 1970, despite an increase in GDP of over 10%, and was much lower than forecasts made in the early 1970s (UK energy consumption peaked in 1973).[52] In effect, the oil crisis triggered the beginning of a 'pervasive, chronic, energy problem'.[53]

## 3.2 The impact of the energy crisis

Government reaction came quickly and there were three basic strands to its response. Firstly, the industrialized countries acted to try and develop a co-ordinated oil policy, and develop a reserve management strategy through the establishment of the International Energy Agency (IEA) in Paris.

Secondly, government responded with a series of attempts to intensify and diversify indigenous energy supply. Research programmes into various

---

[52] G. Leach, C. Lewis, F. Romig, A. van Buren and G. Foley, *A Low Energy Strategy for the United Kingdom*, Science Reviews, International Institute for Environment and Development, London, 1979.

[53] W. Haefele, J. Anderer, A. McDonald and N. Nakicenovic, *Energy in a Finite World*, Ballinger, Cambridge, Massachusetts, 1981, p. 2.

alternative sources of energy were set up in the UK and elsewhere (particularly in those countries suffering a high degree of oil import dependency – most of the OECD, but France, Japan and Italy in particular). The programmes aimed at providing for low-cost future energy supplies that were abundant and secure. In the UK, coal once again came to be seen as central to energy policy – something which the UK coal miners realized quickly in 1974 as they began an important political strike – while exploration and development of indigenous oil and gas resources were stepped up. In the meantime, support grew rapidly for R&D expenditure on a range of alternative technologies including: fast breeder nuclear reactors, advanced coal-fired plants, combined heat and power, nuclear fusion and various renewable energy technologies.[54] Distinct positions were staked out around particular strategies or technologies and the debate about energy futures grew in both intensity and polarity.

Thirdly, government began seriously contemplating the structure of energy demand – focusing on the reasons why energy was actually needed. Conservation programmes were put in place exhorting people to use less, and a vibrant community of researchers in the field of energy demand analysis and forecasting emerged.[55] The UK was one of many countries including Japan, France, USA, Sweden, Australia which attempted to introduce energy conservation programmes to reduce costs, reduce balance of payments problems, and ensure that energy was not being wasted. The need for greater energy consciousness and improvements in energy management became commonly understood and accepted. Many large organizations appointed an energy manager to make sure that energy concerns were integrated into decisions about change and future investments.[56]

Meanwhile, the community of energy policy analysts which had formed began having an impact on the way energy planning in government was approached. The new and uncertain environment called for the development of a new set of policy and analytical tools to deal with the different circumstances

---

[54] For a contemporary review see Department of Energy, *Energy Research and Development in the UK*, Energy Paper Number 11, HMSO, London, 1976.

[55] National Economic Development Office, *Energy Conservation in the United Kingdom*, HMSO, London, 1974.

[56] For example, in 1975, the Institute of Directors in London sponsored a special publication in association with the Department of Energy on *Energy Saving*, Institute of Directors, London, 1975.

and fresh concerns. In particular, developments in three crucial areas of energy policy analysis – energy accounting; energy conservation and efficiency policy; and energy futures analysis – deserve further scrutiny for their possible relevance to transport.

### 3.3 Conceptualizing energy: information and measurement

Envisioning energy can be a complex and difficult task, while measuring the amount of energy used in the economy has never been simple. Energy is a difficult scientific concept and has a muddled socio-technical meaning.[57] The events of the early 1970s helped to fuse together the scientific and the policy understanding of the energy concept.[58] In turn, this had an important effect on the way data about energy uses were measured and how information was introduced into policy-making. The evolution of energy as a scientific and policy concept can be summarized as follows:

- *scientific:* substance → heat → work → mathematical construct;[59]
- *policy:* biomass (wood) → coal → fuel and power → energy → heat/light/ movement, etc.

---

[57]A report by the Department of Environment: *Attitudes to Energy Conservation in the Home*, HMSO, London, 1991, found that the concept of energy was poorly understood by many people.

[58] The fusion of scientific and policy cultures and the cross-fertilization of ideas between them was intense. For example, it spawned a unique brand of energy policy analysis – known as 'energy analysis' (EA). Although the culture of EA did not last long – it had all the problems of an indeterminate social science plus those of an overly reductionist science – it was an important development which has direct implications for the future development of transport thinking. For an example of the take-up of energy analysis see R. Herendeen and J. Tanaka, 'Energy Cost of Living', *Energy*, Vol. 1, 1976, pp. 165–178. For problems with the application of energy analysis to agriculture see M. Jones, 'Analysis of the Use of Energy in Agriculture – Approaches and Problems', *Agricultural Systems*, Vol. 29, 1989, pp. 339–355. For the demolition of EA on the grounds of severe methodological problems, particularly with respect to where system boundaries began and ended, see G. Leach, 'Net Energy Analysis – Is It Any Use?', *Energy Policy*, Vol. 3, No. 4, 1975, pp. 332–334. Although energy analysis is now rarely undertaken, it has been influential in developing ideas about the quality of energy – see M. Bejan, 'A Supply-Side Approach to Energy Policy', *Energy Policy*, Vol. 10, No. 2, 1982, pp. 153–157.

[59] See e.g. P. Mirowski, *More Heat Than Light*, Cambridge University Press, Cambridge, 1989.

We only need to note here that the scientific evolution of the energy concept has been dynamic. Our understanding of energy policy – the philosophy behind governments' approaches to decision making on energy issues – has been changing since before the industrial revolution. Before it was energy policy it was fuel and power policy. Before that it was mines policy and at a stage much before that, wood policy.[60] The relatively recent adoption of the term 'energy policy' itself represents a significant change in the way government viewed the interaction between different fuels and conversion technologies. The 1973 oil crisis played an important part in rationalizing this process further. As oil became scarce, inevitably the question was asked, 'well what is it that we need the oil for – are there other ways of delivering the heat, light and power that are required?' Indeed, this shifted attention to the services/ uses (e.g. light, heat and movement) that energy provided.

Two developments in particular are important from today's transport perspective:

- the existence of common units to aggregate and compare the contribution of different fuels to the balance of overall energy needs;
- a distinction between overall (primary) and end-use (useful) measures of energy consumption.

As governments pondered their energy futures in the broadest perspective, it quickly became clear that there was a need for an accounting system which could capture changes throughout the whole energy economy and not just selected parts of it. The practice of using common measures of overall energy consumption (e.g. tonnes of oil equivalent) to incorporate a range of different fuels aggregated across various types of use was a useful accounting innovation. The IEA summarized the advantages of such a measure as follows:

Analysis of energy policy problems requires a comprehensive presentation of basic statistics in original units such as tons of coal and kilowatt hours

---

[60] General shortages of wood began to occur in England from the end of the fourteenth century onwards, leading to the search for some other fuel: coal – see G.F. Ray, 'Energy Economics – A Random Walk in History', *Energy Economics*, Vol. 1, No. 2, 1979, pp. 139–143.

of electricity. The usefulness of such basic data can be considerably improved by putting them in a single common unit suitable for uses such as estimation of total energy requirements, forecasting and the study of substitution and conservation.[61]

Different fuels could be compared in terms of their energy content: even though, for example, coal, nuclear and renewable energy sources are fundamentally very different, they can be compared in terms of the central unifying concept of their having an equivalent energy content.[62] This was particularly important in view of the complex flow of energy in the economy from primary source through to end-use. Aggregating the contribution of each fuel to overall energy supply and use made it possible to assess the energy situation as a whole, where the relative impact of individual proposals or changes could be measured in their widest context and at different stages of production and consumption. The primary measure of energy consumption – the measure which includes all commercial energy inputs into the economy – has become a familiar and valuable indicator within the field of energy, especially when it is combined with other macroeconomic indicators such as GDP or population.[63] Although the measure of 'useful energy consumption' – which measures the actual productive work which energy users finally derive from the energy which is delivered to them – is not commonly used as an economy-wide measure, it is still a valuable concept, particularly with regard to efforts to improve the efficiency of energy use. The tools of macroeconomic energy analysis became an important input to the new approaches towards energy futures analysis and the foundation (if somewhat crude) upon which government attempts to improve energy efficiency were to be judged.[64]

---

[61] OECD, *Energy Balances of OECD Countries: 1960/74*, IEA/OECD, Paris, 1976.

[62] See Foley, *The Energy Question*. However, while common energy units were good for aggregating overall quantities of energy, they were not able to deal with the quality of energy sources.

[63] For example, as a tool for policy evaluation see Department of Trade and Industry, *Digest of Energy Statistics 1993*. For its use in international comparisons of energy efficiency see T. Morovic, G. Gerritse, G. Jaeckel, E. Jochem, W. Mannsbart, H. Poppke and B. Witt, *Energy Conservation Indicators II*, Springer Verlag, Berlin, 1989.

[64] For example, OECD, *Energy Policies of IEA Countries: 1991 Review*, OECD, Paris, 1992.

## 3.4 UK energy conservation and energy efficiency policy

One of the UK government's immediate policy responses to the 1973 oil crisis was to establish an energy conservation policy. On 9 December 1973, it launched an Energy Saving Programme, marking the beginning of a demand-oriented response to the oil price increases.[65] The programme encouraged individuals and industry to use less energy in order to shield energy users from high energy costs and conserve what were thought to be scarce fossil fuel resources. In 1974, an influential government think-tank – the Central Policy Review Staff – concluded that there was wide scope for energy savings in transportation, electricity generation, domestic energy use and industrial energy use.[66] In the same year a second influential report on energy conservation made further recommendations to the government which responded with an interim programme for energy conservation which included: the appointment of an Advisory Council on Energy Conservation (ACEC); the establishment of the Energy Technology Support Unit (ETSU); and the creation of the Energy Audit and Thrift schemes.[67]

The government continued to promote energy conservation throughout the remainder of the 1970s. In 1977, the 'Save It' campaign was extended for another three years and a dedicated Energy Conservation Division within the Department of Energy was established. However, by the early 1980s – and after a second oil crisis in 1979 – the immediate threats of oil shortages and long-term high oil prices had subsided. Energy conservation – a short-term reaction to reduce immediate dependency on oil and to shield the economy from the effects of high oil prices – was displaced by a more strategic concept of energy efficiency. The 1982 review of how the government had handled energy conservation led to the establishment in 1983 of the Energy Efficiency

[65] Strictly speaking, a form of energy conservation policy had already been in place for some years. The development of energy efficiency policy, however, can be traced back to the formation in 1954 of the National Industrial Fuel Efficiency Service, a non-profit-making company sponsored by the fuel and power industries to promote fuel saving in industry. In addition to consultancy work, it provided advice and services to all non-domestic fuel users in a variety of forms, from 'spot' inspection to full-scale heat and power surveys and regular visits on a contract basis. See the yearly government review: HMSO, *Britain: An Official Handbook*, HMSO, London, 1968.
[66] Central Policy Review Staff, *Energy Conservation*, HMSO, London, 1974.
[67] National Economic Development Office, *Energy Conservation in the United Kingdom*.

Office (EEO) within the Department of Energy.[68] Energy efficiency was seen as part of a wider strategy to promote general economic efficiency in addition to the efficient use of energy resources. Whereas conservation had concentrated on doing without, energy efficiency was marketed as saving money – 'getting more for your monergy'. Energy efficiency was therefore promoted as cost-effective energy saving in the form of the simple message that improved energy efficiency reduced energy bills.

An important step in the development of energy efficiency policy was the adoption by the Secretary of State for Energy in 1983 of a national target to improve national energy intensity – the ratio of total primary energy consumption to GDP – by 20% within 10 to 15 years. The use of an aggregate indicator as a policy target is still part of policy today.[69] It provided a quantified macroeconomic objective that government needed in order to measure its progress. Energy conservation and energy efficiency goals were pursued through three main strategies: information programmes; financial incentive programmes; and regulatory programmes. A brief summary of some of these measures implemented in the UK and elsewhere under each of these areas is given below in Box 3.1.[70]

The rationale for energy efficiency programmes in the UK is now based upon a broad set of strategic macroeconomic criteria including: the need to slow down resource depletion; increased supply security; improved economic competitiveness; enhanced social and welfare policy; and environmental improvements.[71]

The parallels between government's attempts to manage demand in the energy sector during the 1970s and 1980s and the emerging attempts to manage demand now in the transport sector are followed up in Chapter 6 of this report.

---

[68] Department of Energy, *How the Government Handles Energy Conservation*, HMSO, London, 1982.
[69] *Sustainable Development: The UK Strategy.*
[70] For an overview of the wider IEA experience, see OECD, *Energy Conservation in IEA Countries*, OECD, Paris, 1987.
[71] J. Chesshire, 'Energy Efficiency Policy Priorities in 1991 and Priorities for the 1990s', *British Annual Energy Review*, 1991, pp. 41–47.

**Box 3.1 General energy conservation and efficiency programmes**

*Information programmes*

- General campaigns informing energy users of the need for, and advantages of, saving energy and reducing energy costs
- Energy audits – to increase awareness of the conservation and efficiency opportunities
- Energy labels and guides for appliances, engines and houses
- Technical handbooks – detailing how to set up energy management systems
- Advisory services – providing on the spot coordination of information on energy services
- Training and education programmes – attempting to instil concepts of energy conservation for present and future energy consumers.

*Financial investment incentives*

- Grants/loans – e.g. insulation grants, grants for energy surveys, loans to industry and public authorities to purchase new equipment
- Tax incentives – present a more comprehensive signal to consumers to encourage investment in energy efficiency – e.g. for investment in new technology.

*Regulations and standards*

- In the domestic sector, building regulations set a range of minimum technical standards – e.g. draught proofing, loft insulation, double glazing. In industry, there are regulations for the inspection of large boilers
- A 20% target for improving UK energy efficiency was adopted in 1983
- Fuel economy standards for new cars
- Appliance efficiency standards.

## 3.5 Energy futures: forecasts, scenarios, top-down and bottom-up

Forecasting techniques had begun to play an increasingly important role within UK energy policy since they were used in the 1967 White Paper on Fuel Policy.[72] This early energy forecasting style tended to be based on 'top-down' (see below) extrapolations of historical trends in basic macroeconomic features of energy and economic systems. By 1970 most energy forecasts were making exponential-type predictions, often ignoring wider political, institutional and ecological implications – in effect, sometimes projecting revolutionary societal change into the future as 'business as usual'.[73] The unexpected quadrupling of oil prices in 1973 created a new and much more uncertain planning environment. A combination of confusion between widely differing forecasts and the problems of dealing with 'oil crisis types' of uncertainty highlighted the need for an alternative approach to energy planning.[74] Figure 3.2 shows how longer-term forecasts of energy consumption for the year 2000 began to tumble as they were put forward over the period 1974–83. It shows the 1970s clearly as a period in which there was immense confusion surrounding energy forecasting.[75]

Lower economic growth was partly responsible for the continued downward revision of the forecasts, but so too were a variety of institutional conflicts which had begun to feed back into an increasingly self-aware energy forecasting community.[76] The political and technical fallout of such immense forecasting errors led to the development and uptake of scenario analysis on a wide scale at the policy level.[77]

---

[72] HMSO, *Fuel Policy*, HMSO, London, 1967.
[73] See e.g. T. Baumgartner and A. Midttun, 'Energy Forecasting: Art, Science and Politics', in T. Baumgartner and A. Midttun (eds), *The Politics of Energy Forecasting: A Comparative Study of Energy Forecasting in Western Europe and North America*, Clarendon, Oxford, 1987, pp. 3–10.
[74] See M. Jones, 'The UK Energy Debate in the 1980s: Cease-fire or New Consensus', *Energy Policy*, Vol. 18, No. 4, 1990, pp. 381–388.
[75]The backlash against forecasting is described in H. DuMoulin and J. Eyre, 'Energy Scenarios: A Learning Process', *Energy Economics*, Vol. 1, 1979, pp. 76–86. The authors quoted an Arab proverb from the *Koran*: 'Those who foretell the future lie, even if they tell the truth'.
[76] See e.g. Baumgartner and Midttun, 'Energy Forecasting: Art, Science and Politics'.
[77] Scenario analysis had already been used in the oil industry for several years – see e.g. P. Wack, 'Scenarios: Uncharted Waters Ahead', *Harvard Business Review*, Vol. 63, No. 5, September/October 1985, pp. 73–89.

# Figure 3.2 UK primary energy demand forecasts for the year 2000

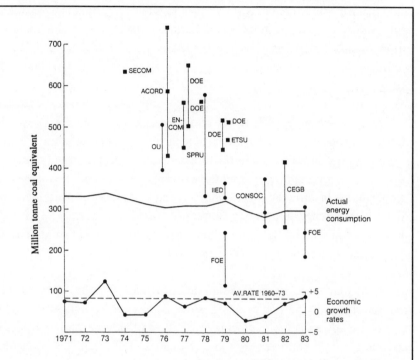

SECOM = Select Committee on Science and Technology (estimates for year 2000 are based on trend extrapolations); OU = Open University, Energy Research Group; ACORD = Advisory Council on Research and Development for Fuel and Power; ENCOM = Energy Commission; DOE = Department of Energy; SPRU = Science Policy Research Unit; ETSU = Energy Technology Support Unit; IIED = International Institute of Environment and Development; FOE = Friends of the Earth; CONSOC = Conservation Society; CEGB = Central Electricity Generating Board

Source: R. de Man, 'United Kingdom Energy Policy and Forecasting: Technocratic Conflict Resolution', in Baumgartner and Midttun, *The Politics of Energy Forecasting: A Comparative Study of Energy Forecasting in Western Europe and North America*, 1987, pp. 110–134 (by permission of Oxford University Press).

Once described as lying somewhere between forecast and fantasy, scenarios span a range of futures which seem plausible under differing sets of assumptions, and hence provide a broader background against which policy assessments can be made.[78] Instead of attempting to predict the most likely

---

[78] A.B. Lovins, *Soft Energy Paths*, Penguin, Harmondsworth, England, 1977.

future, scenario analysis aimed to generate a range of credible futures which could develop – to examine 'what if' questions and to evaluate the sensitivity of the future to changes in certain parameters and therefore anticipate key turning points. Foley describes how the technique overcame the problems of traditional forecasting procedures:

One way of dealing with the problem of energy planning is to construct alternative 'scenarios'. These are imagined pictures of the future which try to envisage the full implications of a particular course of action. Thus, a high-energy scenario would try to imagine how people would actually use extra energy and would examine the social, economic and environmental implications of providing it. In constructing a scenario in which society depended on renewable energy sources, it would be necessary to look at how this might be brought about and what changes would be required in employment patterns, urban life, transport and so forth.[79]

As particular scenarios became an accepted part of policy debates, they were referred to by particular names such as 'low' or 'technical fix' and as such were an extremely effective analytical device and method of communication.[80] However, as scenarios emerged at the policy level, they tended to become used by interest groups and other organizations to pursue their own goals. Lovins sums up some of the frustrations that the new technique created:

Unfortunately the word 'scenario' has lately been robbed of specificity by those unfamiliar with its original use in the film industry. Properly, it refers to a description of how future events unfold, described chronologically and at least qualitatively in sufficiently vivid detail that readers can readily imagine themselves participating in the events it describes. People who find it useful to have a word for this concept should defend it from those who have forgotten how to say 'projection', 'forecast',

[79] Foley, *The Energy Question*.
[80] See M. Jones, C. Hope and R. Hughes, 'A Multi-Attribute Value Model for the Study of UK Energy Policy', *Journal of the Operational Research Society*, Vol. 41 No. 10, 1990, pp. 919–929.

'plan', 'program', 'prediction', 'sketch', 'outcome', 'future', 'prospect', 'trend', 'proposal', 'development' etc.[81]

Scenarios were not exempt from controversy – they too had their limitations. Scenarios were as detailed as those who created them wished them to be – the more detailed they were, the more internal and external consistency they required and the greater effort needed in their creation. The scenario technique, however, quickly became used predominantly as a holistic way both of identifying possible 'patterns' of future development, and as a method for expressing and examining a vision of a desired future.[82] Used in this way, scenario analysis becomes a way of 'backcasting' rather than forecasting. Backcasting is explicitly normative and involves working backwards from a particular desired future end-point to the present, to determine its plausibility and the policy and other conditions that could give rise to it. Whereas good forecasts are meant to converge upon the most likely future, good backcasts can be expected to diverge, to reveal some of the policy implications of and prerequisites for alternative futures.[83]

The use of scenarios and backcasts led to the emergence of several different views about how energy policy might or could evolve which often were linked to the method used to construct the scenarios.[84] In particular, a distinction between 'top-down' and 'bottom-up' modelling was central to the process of developing scenarios. Top-down models are broadly characterized by their emphasis on what is akin to macroeconomic modelling – embodying prices and economic growth as the main determinants of energy use – while bottom-up models are characterized by their focus on the structure of how demand

---

[81] Lovins, *Soft Energy Paths*, p. 65.
[82] See Leach et al., *A Low Energy Strategy for the United Kingdom*, p. 9. They describe their work as emerging largely as a direct challenge to the 'technological optimists' of the nuclear and other supply industries.
[83] J. Bridger Robinson, 'Energy Backcasting: A Proposed Method of Policy Analysis', *Energy Policy*, Vol. 10, No.4, 1982, pp. 337–344.
[84] For example: Energy Project of the Ford Foundation, *A Time to Choose: America's Energy Future*, Ballinger, Cambridge, Massachusetts, 1974; P. Chapman, *Fuel's Paradise*, Penguin, Harmondsworth, 1975; Workshop on Alternative Energy Strategies, *Energy: Global Prospects 1985–2000*, McGraw-Hill, New York, 1977; and Lovins, *Soft Energy Paths*.

changes but leave out prices and new end-uses.[85] In many cases the differences between the higher and lower projections which were made about energy growth in the 1970s can be accounted for by the difference in the two approaches. The energy experience has been that top-down models tended to overestimate growth, partly because they relied on overestimates of GDP and ignored structural changes and saturation of certain types of energy use. In the UK, a study led by Gerald Leach – one of the most influential scenario analyses – identified a future based on a 'low energy strategy'.[86] Using detailed bottom-up assumptions about the future patterns of energy use and energy efficiency, it challenged the widespread belief that the coupling of energy and economic growth had to continue and marked a historic turning point in the evolution of energy futures analysis.[87] Chapter 7 of this report explores how transport forecasting and futures analysis might learn from this past experience of planning in the energy sector.

Much of the analysis of energy policy which was carried out during the 1970s implicitly assumed a much greater role for government intervention and regulation than has actually been the case – the Conservative government took power in 1979 committed to reducing its involvement with long-term energy planning and releasing market forces. Indeed, the speech by the Secretary of State for Energy at Cambridge in 1982 where he announced 'I do not see the Government's task as being to try and plan the future shape of energy production and consumption' signalled the end of an important phase of the development of UK energy policy analysis, largely unrealized in terms of the practical implementation of the ideas which had developed.[88]

---

[85] M. Grubb (ed.), *Energy Policies and the Greenhouse Effect*, Vol. 2, *Country Studies and Technical Options*, Royal Institute of International Affairs, London, 1991.

[86] Leach et al., *A Low Energy Strategy for the United Kingdom*, p. 9.

[87] It has since turned out that the Leach low scenario was very close to actual energy consumption levels, albeit from a quite different set of structural economic and-technical changes to those which were proposed. UK energy consumption in 1990 was 354 million tonnes of coal equivalent, just less than Leach's 358 projected and much less than the 525 that the Department of Energy had proposed.

[88] Department of Energy, *Speech on Energy Policy*, Energy Paper Number 51, HMSO, London, 1982, p. 1. A strong dismissal of the Leach study was published as: United Kingdom Atomic Energy Authority, *An Analysis of the Low Energy Strategy for the United Kingdom*, Energy Discussion Paper Number 1, HMSO, London, 1980.

# Chapter 4

## Using the Analogy Between Energy and Transport

> *Like energy, transport plays a central role in economic development. Passenger and freight miles can be used like megawatt hours to indicate economic activity and are seen by many as yardsticks of prosperity.*
>
> ERNST U. VON WEIZSÄCKER, *EARTH POLITICS*,
> ZED BOOKS, LONDON, 1994, P.66

Analogies are good at generating valuable insights about new or unfamiliar problems. But they can also generate trivial, unhelpful or even false conclusions. Their usefulness tends also to be subjective – as de Bono points out, good analogies are determined by the life they take on in the mind of the individual.[89] Before exploring the policy implications of the parallels between energy and transport in more detail, it is worth spending a little time unpacking the nature of the similarities between them and pointing out some of the differences – bringing out some of the strengths and limitations of the analogy.[90]

### 4.1 Limitations and basis of the analogy

It is invariably easier to highlight differences between two systems than it is to point to the similarities – and energy and transport are no exceptions.[91] One key difference in particular is worth stressing. The existence of international energy markets gave the energy problem a dimension that is largely missing from the transport problem (although there are international passenger

---

[89] de Bono, *Lateral Thinking*.

[90] The usefulness of this kind of cross-sector analogy ought ultimately to be judged by its impact. This process relies heavily on both implicit and explicit comparison.

[91] M.L. Kohn, 'Cross-National Research as an Analytic Strategy', *American Sociological Review*, Vol. 52, 1987, pp. 713–731.

and freight markets, these are not the principal source of most transport problems). This international dimension of the energy problem was an important feature of the energy debate and, as a result, limits the analogy between energy and transport in three ways. Firstly, energy policy had direct, proven and accepted links with macroeconomic policy including implications for the balance of payments and employment. The oil price exerted much influence on government decision making and acted as a direct mechanism for stimulating actions on the part of government, business and individuals. The one market in the transport sector which could possibly have the same effect as the oil price is the market for road space through road pricing. However, road space is not currently priced and even if it were, the market would not be subject to influence from international political events. Secondly, there is no direct corollary in transport policy for the fears over the security of international energy supply that existed post 1973. Perhaps the notion of a 'gridlock' jamming urban areas as a result of a particular set of incidents or congestion and strangling industrial competitiveness comes nearest to the concept of fear or anxiety in transport. Thirdly, the environmental pressures which help fuel today's transport problem were not given as much attention in the debate about energy policy.[92] Since the mid-1970s, environment policy has gradually evolved into an influential area of public policy in its own right and from the late 1980s onwards has steadily become a defining issue within the transport problem, particularly via concerns over local air pollution and the greenhouse effect.[93]

On the surface, there is a broad pattern of resemblance between energy and transport. Transport in the 1990s is strikingly similar to energy as it was in the 1970s – preoccupation with increasing supply is distracted by some measures attempting to manage demand. The dominant approach to energy

---

[92] Early environmental concern in the energy sector centred on the side-effects of nuclear power and the impacts of large oil tanker spills. This is in fact a good example of the strong links and therefore confusion which can arise in comparing energy and transport. Oil tanker spills were seen as disasters related to the transport of energy, not as related to the cars and trucks which produced the demand for oil in the first instance.

[93] See e.g. M. Fergusson, C. Holman and M.Barrett, *Atmospheric Emission from the Use of Transport in the United Kingdom*, Earth Resources Research/World Wildlife Fund for Nature, London, 1989.

and transport policy always has been and still is, by default, supply driven. However, the 1973 oil crisis certainly marked the start of a new emphasis on energy management (albeit limited) while reactions to the 1989 UK road building programme may also have marked the beginning of a distinct long-term phase of demand management entering UK transport policy.[94]

By 1994, attempts to implement the spirit of environmental sustainability across the whole of the economy significantly reduced the apparent lag between policy developments within the two sectors. Both sectors have recently come under substantial social cost scrutiny and form central parts of the UK government's response to sustainable development.[95]

However, while from the environmental perspective, the sectors appear to be at similar stages of development, there is a vital difference between them. Various strategic attempts to diversify and manage energy demand had been underway for two decades in the energy sector before they were proposed in transport. Where they have been achieved, technical and 'good housekeeping' energy efficiency improvements have already reduced the environmental impact of the energy sector without beginning to rely on social costing to further advance these improvements.[96] Social costing in the transport sector might be more effective if the transport sector, too, had made obvious and straight-forward efficiency improvements – 'good road keeping'.[97] At a deeper level, this and the remaining chapters in this report demonstrate that the sectors have yet more in common with each other.

Energy is not transport. Of course, at the most basic level, this is obvious, but it can make comparisons between the nature of the two derived demands conceptually difficult – after all, they both already are abstract concepts.

---

[94] For example, compare the rationales for a move towards demand management in transport – Department of Environment and Department of Transport, *Planning Policy Guidance Note 13* – and in energy 20 years earlier – National Economic Development Office, *Energy Conservation in the United Kingdom*.

[95] *Sustainable Development: The UK Strategy.*

[96] The recent imposition of VAT on domestic fuel and power (formerly zero VAT rated) will also help energy efficiency.

[97] A new culture of constrained road capacity would involve considerable psychological change. Social and industrial structures have evolved in a road space-rich environment (though not always with good-quality roads).

Energy, and much transport, are derived demands in the sense that they are needed to provide more basic needs – energy provides heat, light and movement, and transport predominantly provides access to work, shops, social and leisure opportunities and the choice of business, industrial and work location.[98] It is not always easy to see how the various surface observations which characterize the analogy relate to each other. For example, high prices and the prospect of limited oil supplies were central features of the energy crisis, while limited availability of road space is seen as central feature of the transport problem – but what significance is there in this? Nor is it obvious what significance there is in the observation that both nuclear power and public transport have played important peripheral and polarizing roles within their respective policy debates or that renewable energy technologies seem to have much more in common with the metabolic forms of transport – walking and cycling (which also rely on renewable energy sources).

It is both inevitable and desirable that these kinds of comparisons will be made either in support or to undermine any suggestion of an analogy between energy and transport. In this respect, it would be helpful to have a more explicit comparative framework within which comparisons between the nature of the two derived demands can be made.

## 4.2 Structural similarities between the energy and transport sectors

Different areas of public policy are given their conceptual structures by the way in which issues within them are categorized and quantified.[99] For example, energy policy is debated from a number of different dimensions – the focus could be types of fuel (coal, oil, electricity, etc.) or types of user (industry,

---

[98] Button, *Transport Economics*. Almost all demand for transport is derived from the opportunities which become accessible with movement – only a tiny minority of journeys (e.g. vacational) could ever be said to have been undertaken for the joy, excitement, romance or sentiment of moving.

[99] Categorization and quantification are often linked to the pattern of commercial transactions taking place, or tangible policy outputs which are readily measurable, and are not necessarily useful. In both energy and transport the quality of statistical data is best at the second level from the top in Figure 4.1. It is the energy carriers which are commercially sold, consumed and metered and it is the transport carriers which are most readily counted, for example from the side of the road.

transport, etc.) or types of end-uses (heat, light, motive power, etc.). Together, these dimensions form a coherent framework within which energy policy is evaluated.

The structures of the energy and transport sectors (Figure 4.1) are each dominated by a number of specific primary supply elements (fuels and transport modes) and a set of end-use demand sectors (uses of energy and transport). The top row of Figure 4.1 depicts the common distinctions between basic fuels, and various transport modes. Analogy can be drawn between the range of fuels or energy carriers, such as electricity, and the different ways of travelling, e.g. by car, walking or bus (the 'transport carriers'), on the second row. The third row down lists the areas that are conventionally associated with the different types of consumption (with energy there are the domestic, industrial, transport and other sectors, and in transport there are the passenger and freight sectors). Finally, the bottom row lists the different end-uses that stimulate the demand for energy and transport in the first instance – in energy these are lighting and cooking etc. and in transport they are travel to, from and in the course of work, education and the search for goods and services.

The figure demonstrates two important features. Firstly, the structure of the energy and transport sectors are strikingly similar – showing a high degree of symmetry – and secondly, the structures are linked by the presence of transport within the energy figure.

These conventional structures emerge primarily from the top-down and bottom-up processes of quantification and statistical reporting within each sector. However, the process of categorization often extends beyond the level of accounting and influences the ways in which problems are perceived, defined and approached. The structural analogy outlined in Figure 4.1 is therefore reinforced by similarities in the ways that energy and transport issues are perceived at various stages in their respective policy processes. The nature of energy and transport problems are often characterized by technical uncertainty and public confusion surrounding the nature of the problems themselves. For instance, in energy policy, there has been some debate about the relative environmental merits of different fuels – for example nuclear compared with coal. In the transport sector, a similar debate has occurred concerning the relative importance of cars and lorries as the major source of congestion and

**Figure 4.1 The structural analogy between energy and transport**

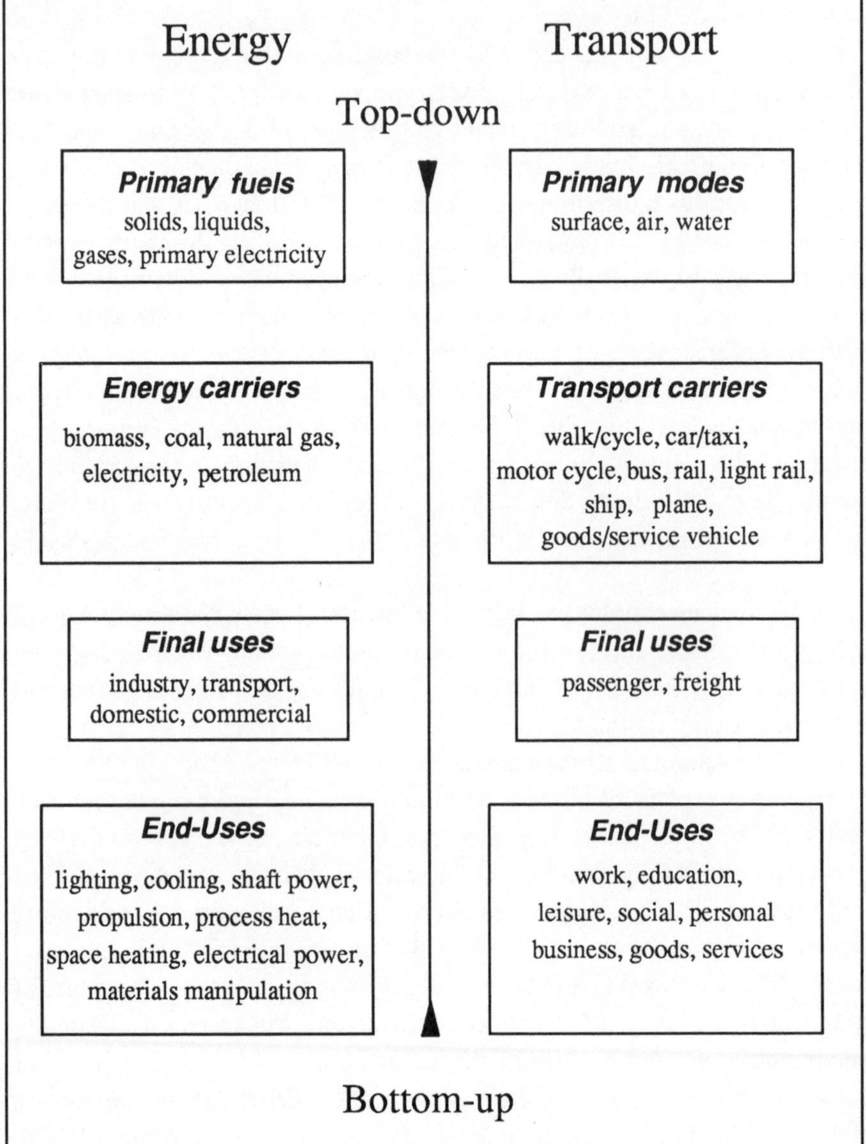

Source: the author.

road damage, and petrol or diesel engines as cleaner.[100] The problem of public understanding of the complexity of transport has also been recognized.[101] The structures in Figure 4.1 are also implicit in the way energy and transport policies are evaluated and monitored. Energy efficiency programmes within the industrial, domestic and commercial sectors are dealt with separately from those relating to transport, while in transport policy analyses, passenger and freight transport are invariably treated separately or exclusively.[102] Finally, experience with the implementation of energy efficiency schemes demonstrates that policies are often best targeted bottom-up on specific end-uses such as space heating or water heating or end-users such as industry, households or commerce, whilst transport demand management has begun to identify and then target specific travel purposes such as travel to work or for leisure, or the superfluous movement of some products and raw materials.[103]

Although the structural analogy is strong and is potentially of great use in making comparisons between the two sectors, it does not, however, guarantee insight. This depends on how the range of possible similarities which the analogy throws up is filtered so that unhelpful, ridiculous or non-sensible conclusions are disregarded. This analysis of the similarities and differences between energy and transport is not exhaustive and the emerging structural analogy is not intended to be presented as rigid or static. Rather, it forms a basis for the more detailed cross-comparisons which are developed in the next three chapters of this report.

---

[100] For example, on the disproportionate contribution of goods vehicles relative to their contribution to traffic see D. Newland, 'Roads to Ruin', *New Scientist,* 15 December 1990, pp. 37–44. One big lorry is capable of doing as much damage to a road surface as 100,000 cars.

[101] On the public's perception of transport problems as involving a great deal of complexity, see Independent Commission on Transport, *Changing Directions.*

[102] On transport being treated separately from other energy sectors see *Sustainable Development: The UK Strategy* and as an example of the fundamental passenger/freight transport divide, see P. Hughes, *Personal Transport and the Greenhouse Effect,* Earthscan, London, 1993.

[103] On the need to target specific uses of energy see J. Bridger Robinson, 'The Proof of the Pudding: Making Energy Efficiency Work', *Energy Policy,* Vol. 19, No. 7, 1991, pp. 631–645. For an example of the way telecommunications as a substitute for transport has been linked to specific journeys purposes see C. Arthur, 'How to Give Up Going to Work', *New Scientist,* 24 October 1992, pp. 23–29.

# Chapter 5

## The Conceptual Analogue: Measuring Transport and Economic Activity

> *If we are to reverse the pattern of environmental degradation that has become one of the hallmarks of the last century we need to start asking ourselves some different questions. Instead of thinking in terms of parts we need to look at the whole.*
>
> *Instead of moving people around, transportation policy all too frequently becomes a matter of moving cars.*
>
> LESTER BROWN, INTRODUCTION TO ZUCKERMANN,
> *END OF THE ROAD*

### 5.1 'Transport': what moves when things change and what changes when things move

People use the word transport as both a noun and a verb.[104] Despite the basic necessity of movement – for everything from basic human survival aid to facilitator of global trade – the concept of transport has a muddled policy meaning. Moreover, the term 'policy' is itself an elusive concept – so the two in tandem create great confusion. The types of quantitative information which are normally used within the transport sector show that transport policy often has a great deal of trouble distinguishing between transport as the movement of vehicles or people or goods – most of the time it implicitly recognizes it as vehicles, and less often people and freight.

This is a common problem in public policy; out of necessity, complex processes are often reduced to numbers where certain criteria – labour, capital and time – are more easily quantified than others – skills, values, quality and

---

[104] For example, 'what transport has been provided?' or 'how can I transport this?' The term 'energy' is used only as a noun.

knowledge. There is always a price to pay in simplifications made to promote and monitor effective action – the balance is between relying on simple aggregated signals for greater clarity and on more detailed 'useful' disaggregated analysis, however, which can stifle action.[105] In practice, the complexity of information used is requisite on purpose. While many kinds of information, in theory, ought to help decision-making, in practice the need for simple and aggregated quantitative information often prevails.[106]

A broad range of transport statistics is currently used to support transport policy analysis. Trying to understand patterns of overall change is very difficult – individual statistics for vehicles, freight and people movements all tell different parts of a bigger story. This chapter explores what happens when the statistical cultures within energy policy analysis are implanted into the transport sector.

*Why aggregate transport statistics?*
The analysis of transport activity within the economy has required the collection of a range of statistics such as total passenger, tonne, and vehicle kilometres moved. These partial measures have emerged as a natural consequence of the very different natures of transport activity across modes and between the passenger and freight sectors. Fundamental as these divisions within the transport sector may seem, there is an important range of perspectives from which such divisions become less important, if not redundant. Different forms of transport are used by the same population, often share the same networks (e.g. roads), take a fraction of the same land area, lubricate the same economy, pollute the same biosphere and rely on the same overall stocks and sources of energy to keep them going.

---

[105] L. Schipper and S. Meyers make a useful distinction on this issue in *Energy Efficiency and Human Activity: Past Trends, Future Prospects*, Cambridge University Press, Cambridge, 1992, p.112. A top-down helicopter view of a forest is useful in getting a feeling for what a forest is in terms of its overall size, and whether it is growing in area, etc., but is of little help in knowing much about what goes on in the forest. A bottom-up view of individual trees is needed to understand much of what determines the life and success of the forest. Both approaches are useful.

[106] For example, complex changes in the economy are reduced to changes in GDP or sometimes in the retail price index, and vital changes in the environment are monitored through human welfare and environmental indices. All indicators have their advantages and problems.

The importance of looking at changes within the transport sector as a whole (in addition to more detailed studies of internal changes) is demonstrated by frequent calls for the 'transport sector' to reduce its environmental impacts such as noise, congestion and emissions of $CO_2$, SOx and NOx, energy consumption, or external environmental and social costs.[107] It is clear that viewed from such broader perspectives, there is a need for measurements which capture the activity throughout the whole transport system and not just selected parts of it. An integrated measure of transport activity across different modes and across both the passenger and freight sectors would be a valuable tool for looking at overall patterns of change in the transport sector. It could be used to explore the efficiency with which the economy *as a whole* uses transport, for contemplating overall future transport requirements and for studying the effects of possible inter-modal and inter-carrier substitutions. As part of the transport transition, it is likely that at some stage the movements of passengers, freight and their carriers will need to be added together in an overall 'helicopter view' and ultimately be held accountable to macroscopic environmental, economic and social constraints within transport networks.

This chapter introduces two new measures of transport activity – a major economy-wide indicator 'Gross Mass Movement' (GMM) and a secondary measure, 'Net Mass Movement' (NMM) which, although it can be defined statistically across the economy, is of most relevance at the carrier level. Both measures rely on a common unit of mass movement – the 'tonne kilometre equivalent'.

The common unit and the two measures are used to describe historic trends in the relationship between overall UK transport activity and economic activity (GDP) over the period 1952–92. Trends in overall economy-wide 'transport efficiency' are shown using a new indicator 'Gross Transport Intensity' (GTI).

## 5.2 Measuring overall transport activity in the economy: gross and net mass movements

The complexity of activities which underlie the use of the term 'transport' are manifest in the broad range of measurements which are used to monitor the

---

[107] See e.g. *Sustainable Development: The UK Strategy*. The chapter on transport (para 26.8) states: 'The transport sector will have to make a contribution to meeting a number of international and domestic environmental targets'.

way people and goods move. Attempting to measure the overall demand for transport with existing statistics is a difficult and frustrating exercise. There are many different kinds of variables, many of which cannot be combined with one another.

Different statistics are collected for different modes (e.g. surface, sea and air) and within those modes for different forms of transport (or 'carriers' – e.g. for surface modes there is the car, bus, bicycle or train). Some statistics focus on the measurement of what is actually being carried (e.g. the quantity and distance of passengers or freight moved) while others measure activity related to the movement of the carrier itself (e.g. the number of car km, HGV km or train km). Although each of these indicators arises as a 'Naturalrechnung'[108] – natural measure – for the measurement of certain types of transport phenomena (e.g. the number of cars or buses on the road or the number of people in them), their use in describing broad trends across the whole transport sector creates methodological and interpretative problems. On what basis should movements of vehicles, passengers or freight be compared? The lack of integration between different statistical measures of transport activity reflects two distinctions in particular. Firstly, there is a fundamental distinction between the movement of people ('passenger transport') and the movement of goods ('freight transport') and secondly there is a basic distinction between the movement of people or goods and the movements of the carriers which propel them.

The first distinction appears to prevent the creation of an aggregate measure for both types of activity. Schipper and Meyers, for example, note:

There is not a good measure of overall activity for transportation....The very different natures of passenger and freight transport make construction of a single indicator impossible.[109]

---

[108] J. Martinez-Allier, *Ecological Economics,* Basil Blackwell, Oxford, 1987.
[109] Schipper and Meyers, *Energy Efficiency and Human Activity: Past Trends, Future Prospects.* This is an important point and is a good example of the energy-transport analogy at work. The authors' focus was on energy, and it is in that context – as part of the energy policy analysis community – that the potential role of an overall measure may have caused them to make this observation.

However, the distinction is not as clear and fundamental as it seems. As Goodwin et al. note, for example:

... in many ways they [passenger and freight movements] are two ends of the same process. Freight travel is concerned with the distribution of goods and a large part of personal travel is related to the production and consumption of the same goods.[110]

The example of a car supermarket shopping trip demonstrates some of the definitional boundaries within the present system of classification. The goods journeys made by HGVs from distribution centres to supermarkets are measured as freight transport, whereas shoppers' journeys from supermarkets are measured solely as passenger transport even though one estimate is that they take home on average 23 kilos of goods each.[111] If the shoppers' average journey back from the supermarket is around 7 km and the distance the goods travel from the distribution centre to the supermarket is say 70 km, then actual freight transportation could be as much as 10% higher in this sector than that reported by the Department of Transport using its current 'tonne kilometre' definitions, and even higher on the basis of freight 'vehicle kilometre' measurements.

There are further anomalies in the methods which distinguish passenger from freight transport. The drivers of goods vehicles and of public transport vehicles are not included in UK transport statistics as passenger transport yet the drivers of cars and taxis are included. Were the carriage of goods vehicle drivers, bus and coach drivers included, the official estimate of total UK passenger movements for 1992 would rise by 17%.[112]

In principle then, there should be scope for common units in transport. But which? The range of units used for measurement is shown in Table 5.1. Seven out of the eight units have drawbacks as potential common units:

[110] P.B. Goodwin, S. Hallett, F. Kenny and G. Stokes, *Transport: The New Realism*. Report to the Rees Jefferys Road Fund for Discussion at the 'Transport – The New Realism' Conference, London, 21 March 1991, p.21.
[111] Ibid.
[112] Department of Transport, *Transport Statistics Great Britain*.

## Table 5.1 Measurements of transport activity

| Measure | Units |
|---|---|
| Passenger kilometres | passenger km |
| Tonne-kilometres (goods moved) | tonne km |
| Vehicle or 'carrier'* kilometres | vehicle km |
| Journeys or trips | number |
| Journey stages | number |
| Tonnes (goods lifted) | tonnes |
| Expenditure | pounds sterling |
| Energy consumption | e.g. tonnes oil equivalent |

*Carrier here is used to describe any sort of transport propulsion technology, e.g. train, ship, plane.

(1) there is no passenger equivalent of freight tonne km (there is, however, a freight equivalent of passenger masses);
(2) vehicle kilometres take no account of the contents of the vehicle either in passenger or freight terms;
(3) the numbers of passenger or freight journeys do not take distance into account;
(4) journey stages do not take account of the distance that the passengers or freight are moved;
(5) goods lifted is only a measure of freight handling;
(6) expenditure on transport is a poor measure of distance or quantity of goods and passengers moved, since this is only part of the link between costs and prices (especially between different modes);
(7) the diversity of technological efficiencies in the energy consumption of different types of carrier and mode means that total annual energy consumption does not always follow mass and distance moved.

Interestingly, however, the three most widely used measures of transport activity (the vehicle kilometre, passenger kilometre and tonne kilometre, each compound two basic criteria – the distance that vehicles, passengers or freight travel and the number of vehicles, passengers or mass of freight which is transported. While all three measures incorporate distance, they relate to three separate quantities: vehicles, passengers and freight. One of the only ways in which the distances and different quantities of vehicles, passengers and freight could be aggregated together is if their masses are used as the integrating factor. This would basically amount to an extension of the goods moved measure of freight activity to cover the movement of passengers, freight and vehicles.[113] There are then, two different ways of measuring overall transport activity. One is to focus on the 'useful' element of the activity – the movement of goods and people which can be thought of as 'net' transport activity (Net Mass Movement – NMM). The other is to consider the total transport activity which includes the carrier – the mass movement of the car, train or whatever else has to be moved as well as the 'useful' component which together form a 'gross' measure of transport activity (Gross Mass Movement – GMM).

The units of NMM and GMM are the same as those traditionally used for measuring freight transport. However, following a similar convention in the energy sector, the units may be expressed as 'tonne kilometre equivalents' (tkme) to signify the conversion of passenger and vehicle movements into their freight equivalents. There is a clear analogy here with energy, and the distinction between useful and primary energy consumption used in the energy sector is similar to the distinction beween net and gross measures of transport activity (Figure 5.1 and 5.2).

Just as the primary measure includes all inputs of energy to the economy, the gross measure of transport activity includes all mass movements in the economy (passengers, freight, carriers). Furthermore, just as the useful measure of energy consumption includes only that energy which actually produces the intended work, the net measure includes only those movements which are

---

[113] Mass transit systems such as trains and planes already make limited use of such an aggregation on mass movement terms. For railways, gross tonne-kilometres hauled is already used as a measure of work – see United Nations, *Annual Bulletin of Transport Statistics For Europe*, UNECE Vol.1, UN, New York, 1993, p. 276. The idea of aggregating passengers, freight and vehicles as 'objects' is also implicit in the analysis of public transport systems efficiency and productivity – see e.g. V.R. Vuchic, *Urban Public Transportation*, Prentice Hall, Englewood Cliffs, 1981, p. 517, which uses a definition of transportation work based on 'the quantity of performed movement computed as the number of transported objects multiplied by the distance over which they are carried'.

**Figure 5.1 Primary and useful measures of energy consumption in the economy**

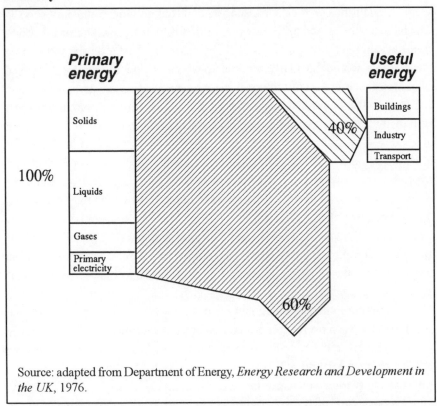

Source: adapted from Department of Energy, *Energy Research and Development in the UK*, 1976.

actually productive (i.e. the movement of passengers and freight and not the carriers). The difference between gross and net amounts to the productive 'losses' from the movement of transport carriers.

The analogy can be extended further to one particular type of productive loss within net activity itself, as a result of the freight transport needs of the 'transport industry' – the amount of freight it takes to keep the economy moving. Fifteen per cent of the road freight activity shown for 1991 in Figure 2.3 and over 20% of total freight transport in the UK are the materials – two-thirds of which is petroleum – which are needed by these transport industries themselves (see Box 5.1).

**Figure 5.2 Gross and net mass movement measures of transport activity in the economy**

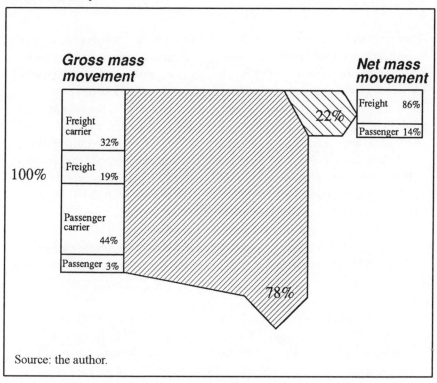

Source: the author.

The energy-transport analogy suggests that GMM is a good indicator of overall trends in transport activity with a considerable power of synthesis. As an aggregate measure, NMM is more limited. The method for calculating GMM and NMM is outlined in Box 5.2.

### 5.3 Micro-interpretations and derivatives of gross mass movement: carrier mass productivity

The performance of transport carriers is measured in many different ways – speed, operating line efficiencies (for public transport) and average utilization – several of which depend on the relationship between overall carrier size and

**Box 5.1 The freight transport demands of the transport industry in Great Britain: 1991***

The demand for transport is met through the involvement of a significant proportion of an economy's industrial and business activity. Each economic activity which is related to the production, maintenance or running of transport infrastructures and technologies constitutes part of an overall 'transport supply industry'. Hence, the demand for mobility is itself responsible for generating part of the overall demand for transport. In the case of freight transport, the contribution of the transport supply industry to overall demand for freight transport in GB in 1991 was considerable – 22% of all freight movements were the transport supply industry's own use of freight transport. Much of this – two-thirds – is the movement of crude petroleum and products, mainly by ship and pipeline, but also by road.

The amount of freight transport activity for the three main categories of materials and commodities which are used by the transport industry is listed below:

| | | |
|---|---|---|
| petroleum products | 31 btkm | (mainly by ship and pipe) |
| crude minerals | 10 btkm | (mainly by road) |
| transport equipment | 6 btkm | (mainly by road) |
| *sub-total of above* | *47 btkm* | |

The sub-total of these three categories, 47 btkm, represents 22% of the total freight activity for 1991 in Great Britain which was 212 btkm. In 1991, supplying the British transport system with its own internal requirements therefore took almost twice as much transport as supplying all the food for people and animals (25 btkm).

* A detailed analysis of this calculation is contained in S.R. Peake, 'Cross-Sector Policy Research: Insights from the UK Energy and Transport Sectors', unpublished PhD thesis, University of Cambridge, 1993.

Sources: Department of Transport, *Transport Statistics Great Britain*, 1993, *Sustainable Development: The UK Strategy*.

**Box 5.2 Method for calculating gross and net mass movements**

Both processes involve converting original statistics on transport activity into common units and then combining these with data on the unladen masses of carriers.

*Gross mass movement (GMM)*

GMM includes the mass movement of people, freight and carriers. Freight statistics are already measured on a net mass moved basis, while statistics on annual passenger kilometres by each mode can be converted into tkme using an assumption about the average mass of a person. Available statistics on total annual carrier kilometres by each transport mode can be transformed into mass movement units by multiplying the number of carrier kilometres for each mode by the average mass of a carrier for that mode. Clearly, not all types of car, train and lorry have the same unladen masses. An estimation of the unladen mass of the *typical* carrier for each mode must be made. This introduces a degree of uncertainty but one which can be minimized so that the results give a reasonably accurate picture of the changes and trends taking place (see Appendix).

*Net mass movement (NMM)*

If, for example, the average passenger weighs 50 kg, then 20 passenger kilometres measured on the NMM basis will count as 1 tonne kilometre equivalent. Total NMM is the sum of the passenger and freight mass movements. The fact that this conversion gives equal importance to 20 passenger kilometres as it does to 1 freight tonne-kilometre illustrates the limitations of NMM as an aggregate measure across passenger and freight, but it still provides a consistent overall indicator of 'useful' transport activity.

carrying capacity.[114] The economy-wide NMM and GMM measures invoke a mass-based measure of the productivity of different carriers. At this micro level, different carriers can be compared in terms of a productivity ratio which indicates 'transport efficiency' by relating useful output to total input.[115] On a mass basis, the transport efficiency of a particular carrier is the carrier mass productivity (CMP), where:

CMP = net mass of passengers or freight /total gross carrier mass.

There are in fact many other ways in which the output and input could be judged, notably by taking into account time, money, labour and even energy. Mass is just one, but it is the one which is of most relevance to the NMM and GMM economy-wide measures.

CMP varies as a function of transport mode and the occupancy or load factor for that mode (Figure 5.3).[116] The data have been estimated for 'typical' transport modes in the UK and are therefore only indicative of the general case – and indeed there are large uncertainties involved in the estimation of average load factors for bulk goods movements, especially by rail and sea.[117] They do, however, provide a good picture of the idea that different carriers perform their useful transport work with differing mass efficiencies.

The length of the bars represents the CMP for that mode at different levels of occupancy or load. The figure shows that CMPs vary in a broad 'U' shape from the metabolic to the motorized transport carriers and on to freight carriers. Walking has a CMP of unity – the maximum possible, since all movement is productive. The more mass that is required to move units of people or goods, the lower the CMP.

---

[114] See Vuchic, *Urban Public Transportation*.

[115] This is just an extension of the general idea of efficiency which can be measured in several ways: see ibid.

[116] This is similar to the concept of specific energy consumption (SEC) for a particular transport mode. SEC is a measure of the amount of energy consumed in carrying one passenger (or one tonne for freight) for one kilometre: see D.J. Martin and R.A.W. Shock, *Energy Use and Energy Efficiency in UK Transport up to the Year 2010*, Department of Energy Efficiency Paper Number 10, HMSO, London, 1989.

[117] see Appendix.

At the typical occupancies observed, cars have a higher CMP ratio than buses, although at maximum occupancies, the CMP ratio for buses is greater by a third. The large unladen masses of passenger trains gives them the lowest CMP ratio – lower even than planes at typical occupancy.[118] The relative advantages of moving freight over passengers is seen in the larger CMPs for the freight modes which vary only slightly at both maximum and 50% load factors between road, rail and water.

## 5.4 Macro-interpretations and derivatives of gross mass movement: environmental impact and economic intensity indicators

*GMM as a proxy for environmental impacts of transport*

There is some intuitive appeal in interpreting GMM as a kind of proxy for the overall environmental impact of transport at the aggregate economy-wide level. However, the broad range of diverse impacts which transport has on the physical and social environment is not easily captured by any single statistic. Impacts vary across transport modes and carriers as well as spatially and temporally according to how and where movements take place.

At the microscopic level, the links between energy consumption, congestion and gross carrier mass, for example, are complex.[119] The data shown in Figure 5.4 give a good indication of the sorts of correlations which exist in the UK for typical classes of carrier. In both Figures 5.4 A and B, the closer to the bottom left-hand corner of the graph the carrier is depicted, the less mass, energy and space intensive it is (i.e. per useful passenger kilometre or for freight modes per useful tonne kilometre). While for a particular carrier, these intensities rise as gross carrier mass increases (with increasing occupancy), they do not always rise with increasing gross carrier mass when different

---

[118] The CMP in this instance is based on a typical conventional 'heavy rail' system. Lighter rapid transit systems such as light urban rail or modern trams are likely to have significantly higher CMP ratios.

[119] Peake, *Cross-Sector Policy Research: Insights from the UK energy and Transport Sectors*. Speed is also important. This is why relatively mass efficient planes (see Figure 5.3) still have considerable environmental impacts. In addition, the combination of mass and speed – momentum – is also a key link between transport and important social impacts such as fear, physical intrusion and accidents resulting in serious injuries.

*The conceptual analogue:*

**Figure 5.3 Carrier mass productivity at typical and maximum occupancies or loads**

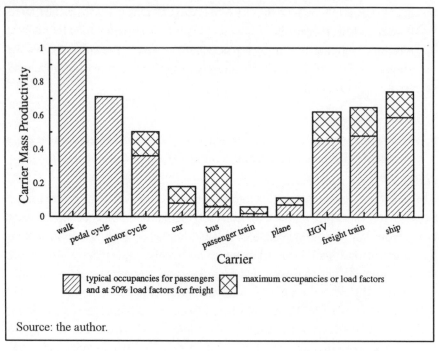

Source: the author.

carriers are compared with each other. At typical occupancies, an average bus, for example, is less energy and congestion intensive compared with an average car, even though the gross carrier mass intensity of buses is greater.

The complexity of the relationships between gross carrier mass and important indicators such as energy consumption and congestion reveal the limitations of interpreting GMM as a proxy for environmental impact at the aggregate level. GMM has the same kind of intuitive appeal as primary energy consumption, which is broadly linked with the overall environmental impact of an energy system, but also suffers from the same kinds of limitations. Like alternative fuel sources, different forms of mass movement have different kinds of impacts on the environment. Different economies with the same overall level of energy and transport consumption can have very different levels of overall environmental impact depending on their energy mixes or transport modal splits. Comparability between different absolute levels of consumption in different economies is therefore limited. Comparisons between rates of change of overall energy consumption or GMM for different economies are a more useful proxy for monitoring the change in overall environmental impact.

The simple and intuitive rule of thumb that lighter transport is better is already implicit in much of current transport thinking. For example, new technologies such as light urban rail systems, personal rapid transport systems and lightweight 'supercars' are all advanced as potential solutions to different transport problems.[120] Of course the metabolic forms of transport – walking and cycling – are the two classic examples of this rule; however, Figures 5.4 A and B show that to a limited extent this also broadly holds for other forms of transport too. Analytical tools such as gross carrier mass and CMPs give what is an already important feature of vehicle design a new, wider and more strategic meaning.[121] The 1973 oil crisis was a key factor in stimulating interest in the idea of making vehicles lighter to reduce their energy consumption.[122] Reductions in gross carrier masses are still seen as a main factor in the improvement of the energy efficiencies of various transport carriers. This is well understood, for example, in airlines where marginal running costs are particularly sensitive to gross take-off weights.[123]

There is an important synthesis of ideas here between attempts to improve vehicle fuel economy and the energy-transport analogy which suggests that

---

[120] See Rocky Mountain Institute, 'Freewheeling: The Coming Supercar Revolution', *RMI Newsletter* Vol. IX(2). S. Nadis, 'High Hopes For Faster Transit', *New Scientist*, 5 March 1994, pp. 28–32.

[121] Vehicle designers and engineers have not always had to consider the weight of a vehicle – as shown by the massive weights of British and American cars in the 1950s and 1960s. For a detailed analysis of weights of British cars – see Peake, 'Cross-Sector Policy Research: Insights from the UK Energy and Transport Sectors', (pp. 62, 65). Prior to the 1973 oil crisis vehicle weight, if anything, was seen in the US as a benefit – see J. Jerome, *The Death of the Automobile*, W.W. Norton, New York, 1972. The Chevrolet Impala was marketed as '3860 LBS. OF SOLID COMFORT' (page 48).

[122] See for example R.H. Essenhigh et al., 'Effect of Vehicle Size and Engine Displacement on Automobile Fuel Consumption', *Transport Research A*, Vol. 13A, 1979, pp. 175–177. See also C.L. Gray and F. von Hippel, 'The Fuel Economy of Light Vehicles', *Scientific American*, 244(5), 1981, pp. 36–47.

[123] D.J Martin and R.A.W. Shock, *Energy Use and Energy Efficiency in UK Transport up to the Year 2010.*

68     *The conceptual analogue:*

## Figure 5.4A Indicative correlation between gross carrier mass and energy consumption: by carrier

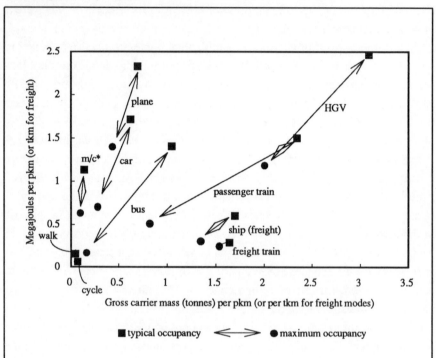

*motor cycle

Sources: The figures for energy consumption used here are derived from data contained in the following: D.J. Martin and R.A.W. Shock, *Energy Use and Energy Efficiency in UK Transport up to yhe Year 2010*, 1989, Department of Energy Efficiency Paper No 10, London: HMSO; CEC, 'The Impact of Transport on the Environment' 1992, COM(92) 46 final; and data based on UK domestic flights supplied by British Airways. Data on 'Passenger Car Units' taken from R.M. Kimber, M. McDonald and N.B. Hounsell, *The Prediction of Saturation Flows For Road Junctions Controlled by Traffic Signals*, 1986, Transport and Road Research Laboratory Research Report 67, TRRL, Bracknell, England.

**Figure 5.4B Indicative correlation between gross carrier mass and road congestion: by carrier**

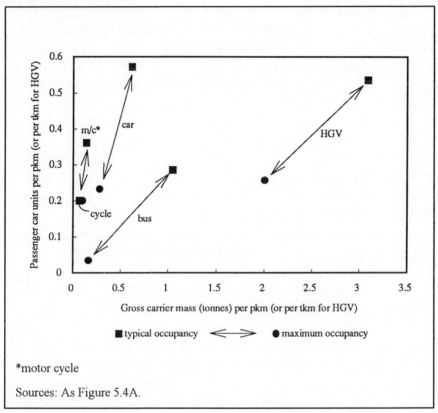

*motor cycle

Sources: As Figure 5.4A.

as well as improving overall fuel efficiency, higher CMPs increase overall transport efficiency.

As a first approximation (if somewhat crude) the link between GMM and overall environmental impact and possibly some social impacts can be used to postulate a rough measure of the 'sustainability' of transport – the higher the level of GMM, the less sustainable the particular pattern of transport activity. Certainly modal switches towards walking and cycling and modal efficiency improvements which, for example, increase carrier occupancies carry with them significant environmental benefits.

GMM can, however, only be a rough guide since the specific environmental impacts of transport at the micro level are dependent on a complex set of factors ranging from the fuel conversion technologies used to the time and place where the activity takes place. One tonne kilometre equivalent of mass movement by rail has very different environmental impacts from the same mass movement by road or air. In principle, the link between GMM and environmental impact could be refined using a matrix of different weightings for particular environmental impacts across different carriers. This would be similar, for example, to the use of carbon coefficients for different fuels and greenhouse effect equivalents for different atmospheric emissions.

*Gross mass movement and economic activity*
The GMM statistic captures all transport movements in the economy – passengers, freight and all types of carrier – in effect, all commercial plus most other transport activity.[124] These movements all have both economic and non-economic costs and benefits attached to them. The analogy between primary energy consumption and GMM suggests that the ratio of gross mass movement to GDP – 'Gross Transport Intensity' (GTI) – would be a useful proxy for changes in national 'transport efficiency' (like its energy counterpart, national energy intensity used to measure changes in 'national energy efficiency'). Of course, the history of energy policy tells us that changes in primary energy intensity can hide several types of underlying structural change – economic, technical and behavioural. Indeed, the distinction between national primary energy intensity and energy efficiency has been made very clear to those for whom this indicator is a useful guide for monitoring progress in this area.[125] The rate at which the economy is heading away from, or towards, sustainability – given the pressures for overall economic activity to continue to grow – can be judged by the rate of change in GTI.

In addition, and as a baseline from which 'useful' economic transport productivity can be judged, NMM can also be combined with GDP to produce

---

[124] All except walk journeys under 1.7 km for which comparable data over long periods are not readily available.
[125] For example, on the implicit psychological effect of viewing changes in national energy intensity as part of an overall energy efficiency league table see National Audit Office, *National Energy Efficiency*, HMSO, London, 1989, p.8.

a measure of Net Transport Intensity (NTI) – indeed derivatives of this concept have already been used as indicators of cross-national differences between transport sectors in a handful of studies.[126]

Gross mass movement and gross transport intensity are highly aggregated statistics. As such they suffer from the same 'health warnings' which have been applied to many aggregate statistics which are used throughout every policy sector. However, it is the well-observed behaviour of actors within the policy process to be self-selective of the types of information they use. Advocates of a particular position choose those statistics which suit the purpose of getting their point of view across, and all parties are capable of accepting, cautioning against or interpreting the use of different types and qualities of information. The principles behind the definition and measurement of the GMM and GTI indicators are new, while the data used in this report to construct them are undoubtedly comparatively poor – many thousands of person years have been used up in developing equivalent indicators for some other social, economic and environmental fields. However, the principle that the increasingly widespread and intensified demands for transport now means that there is an important supporting role for aggregate indicators of the relationship between overall transport demands and other environmental and economic indicators is a highly intuitive and appealing one.

The lessons of the history of energy are very clear with respect to the further development and use of aggregate indicators such as GMM and GTI for policy analysis. They are that such indicators should not be used, or relied upon as a substitute for more detailed bottom-up data analysis – on the contrary, they back up the argument that there needs to be a better understanding of the forces which lie behind them.

---

[126] Net intensities have already been employed in the following analyses: Greenpeace, *Dead End Road: Klimaschutz im europaischen Guterverkehr – Ein Greenpeace Szenario*, Freiburg, EURES, 1992; A. Grubler and N. Nakicenovic, *Evolution of Transport Systems: Past and Future*, IIASA Research Report 91-8, IIASA, Laxenburg, 1991; World Bank, 'China: The Transport Sector', Annex 6 to *China: Long-Term Development Issues and Options*, The World Bank, Washington DC, 1985; Schipper and Meyers, *Energy Efficiency and Human Activity: Past Trends, Future Prospects*.

## 5.5 Aggregate transport trends in the UK: 1952–1992

The trends in overall NMM and GMM by carrier over the last four decades for the UK are shown in Figure 5.5.[127] The results of the analysis are sensitive to a range of uncertainties brought about by the method used to construct the indicators and in the values of some key parameters. However, by reducing the uncertainty surrounding those parameters to which the NMM and GMM were most sensitive, the accuracy of the estimates of total annual mass movements over the period was made significantly better (see Appendix). NMM is sensitive only to the value chosen for the mass of a passenger and luggage – uncertainty here is not important as its contribution to overall GMM is negligible. The data for the trends in UK GMM presented here, however, should be treated as a good first estimate based on the limitations of the methodology used and the quality of information available. There are many further avenues which need to be followed to develop the robustness of the method and data – the aim here is to put the idea across that overall changes in transport activity can be described in a single measure and that the change in this measure is a useful indicator for policy analysis.

To put the overall change in GMM into context, relative to population trends in the UK, the increase in the amount of movement generated in the economy over the last four decades is considerable. In 1952, all mass movements – passengers, freights and carriers – taken together were equivalent to each person in the UK – man, woman and child – driving a loaded 14-tonne goods vehicle 1.4 km each day. By 1992, the increase in gross mass movement amounted to each person in the UK – man, woman and child – driving a fully loaded 38-tonne goods vehicle 1.4 km each day.

Key features in the overall trend for UK GMM include:

- GMM has trebled in 40 years from 350 btkme in 1952 to 1,070 btkme in 1992;
- total passenger activity rose from 43% of GMM in 1952 to 48% by 1992 – the figure shows clearly that in terms of mass movement overall UK transport activity can be described as half passenger and half freight;

---

[127] In this report, only UK domestic passenger and goods movements are incorporated (i.e. international travel, or components of it in UK territory are not).

**Figure 5.5 Passenger and freight components of gross and net mass movements in the UK: 1952–1992**

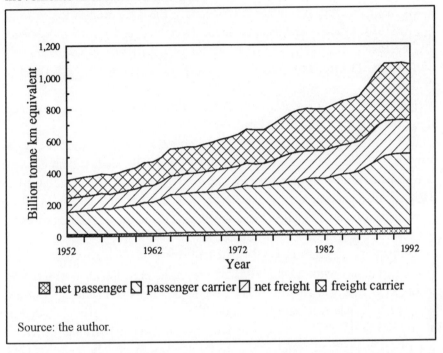

Source: the author.

- over 90% of GMM passenger activity are carrier movements – this reflects the relative mass inefficiency of personal transport in particular, but powered transport in general;
- around 60% of GMM freight activity has been carrier movements (actually 57% rising to 63% in 1992);
- the ratio of overall national transport mass productivity – NMM/GMM – declined from 0.29 in 1952 to 0.23 in 1992, indicating a 20% decrease in the useful productivity of transport movements within the economy.

Two important conclusions may be drawn from Figure 5.5. Firstly, it reveals that 77% of all mass movements is the incidental movement of carriers. Moving people and goods can be productive; moving carriers is not itself productive. Straight away, this suggests that the growth in GMM could in fact be curbed or stopped by substituting more of the incidental movements of carriers for the expected growth in people and goods movements, through modal switching and a range of efficiency measures. Secondly, the 20% drop in the ratio of NMM/GMM indicates that incidental (and unproductive) transport movements are increasing at a faster rate than useful passenger and freight transport movements. The mass productivity of transport in the UK has been steadily declining.

Figure 5.6 shows the contribution of each of the different passenger and freight modes to overall GMM in 1992.

HGV and car-based transport each accounted for a third of all mass movements. The rest is divided between the remaining modes. Walking and two-wheeled transport can only just be seen – although these account for 32% of all journeys, they make hardly any contribution to GMM. Rail movements (mostly passenger) accounted for 13% of the total, and domestic waterborne transport for 8% of the total.

The resulting changes in GMM and NMM over the period 1952–92 can now be combined with GDP (1985 factor cost) to show the long-term trends in UK GTI and NTI (Figure 5.7).[128] Figure 5.7 reveals a striking contrast between NTI (relatively constant) and GTI which begins to increase steadily after 1973. Total NTI is fairly constant over the period at around 0.7 tkme per £1 GDP (85% of which is due to freight movement). In contrast, GTI fluctuated at around 2.6 tkme per £1 until the early 1970s but then increased from 2.6 tkme per £1 in 1973 to 3.1 tkme per £1 in 1992 (a 19% increase). This increase was split roughly half and half between passenger and freight movements. Hence in 1992, for every £1 of GDP generated in the UK, 3.1 tonnes of passengers/freight/carrier were moved through 1 km, made up of 1.5 tonnes of passengers and passenger carriers and 1.6 tonnes of freight and freight carriers.

Figure 5.7 provides a valuable new perspective at the broadest level for envisioning the overall problem that transport is facing. The continuation of the trend shown in Figure 5.7 would mean further increases in gross mass Movement per unit GDP which, in a growing economy reluctant to adopt

---

[128] Combining GB transport statistics with UK GDP (statistics for Northern Ireland cannot easily be separated out) introduces a small systematic error (not more than 2% at most) in this calculation.

**Figure 5.6 Gross mass movement in the UK: 1992**

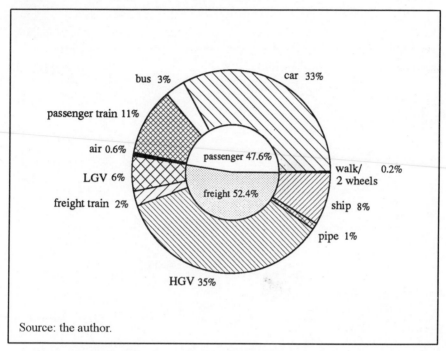

Source: the author.

significantly different patterns of mobility and freight consumption/distribution, can only result in further increases in the social, economic and environmental costs of transport. The 19% increase in GTI over the period is a stark indication of the rate at which transport is heading away from sustainability.

Transport demand management must at some stage address this central problem of year on year increases in mass movement. Historically, after some stage, economies become less intensive in the use of a whole range of raw materials, energy, labour and other primary inputs. However, unlike UK national primary energy intensity for example, which has decreased by 40% since 1952, GTI has continued to rise by half as much (Figure 5.8). This sharp contrast indicates the different stages of development which the economy is at with respect to its use of energy and transport.

Also shown in Figure 5.8 (the dotted line) is the ratio between the amount of energy used for transport and GDP over the period. This curve also began to

**Figure 5.7 Gross and net transport intensities: 1952–1992**

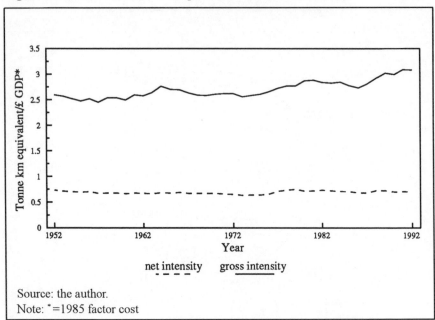

Source: the author.
Note: *=1985 factor cost

rise from the mid-1970s, suggesting an aggregate correlation between GMM and energy consumption despite the modal differences.

The comparison of the aggregate indices for energy and transport raises an obvious question – why has the economy become less energy intensive, yet not less transport-intensive? The history of energy policy tells us that through structural economic changes, and in some cases specific government actions, it is possible for the intensity of at least one other derived demand to decline. If transport (another largely derived demand) intensity were to begin to decline, for example, in a way similar to that in which energy intensity has declined over the last four decades, then higher levels of economic activity could be sustained while reducing the mass movement in the economy.

## 5.6 Conclusions

Analysing the cumulative impacts and importance of change in overall transport activities at the broadest level requires new ways of measuring

**Figure 5.8 Gross transport and primary energy intensities in the UK: 1952–1992**

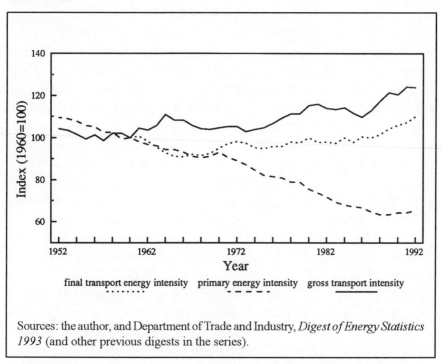

Sources: the author, and Department of Trade and Industry, *Digest of Energy Statistics 1993* (and other previous digests in the series).

aggregate transport activity whether this is people, their goods and services or the propulsion systems which carry them. Measuring transport activity on a mass movement basis provides a new and potentially powerful description of changes in the efficiency with which the various transport modes and carriers are used throughout the whole economy and contribute to the balance of overall transport needs.

Viewing transport activity in this way provides fresh insights into the broad patterns of change within the transport sector. Taking the UK as an example, 77% of all mass movement in 1992 was the incidental movement of carriers and not people or goods, and the gap between NMM and GMM is widening. The ratio of GMM to GDP has also been increasing. GTI has grown at a faster rate than the economy over the last forty years, resulting in a 19% increase in gross transport intensity between 1952 and 1992. GTI has grown significantly, yet NTI – the useful component – has stayed almost constant. These data reveal declining mass productivity in the transport sector.

Just as changes in primary energy intensity have been used to measure changes in national 'energy efficiency' within the macroeconomy, GTI is the natural indicator of changes in macroeconomic 'transport efficiency' – it is the only self-consistent physical definition of transport throughout the whole economy. The contrast between the UK's rising transport intensity and declining energy intensity provides a stark indication of the uphill climb now facing the transport sector as a whole if past trends are to continue.

Great care will be required to develop the methodology and information needed to support the wider usage of measures such as GMM and GTI, particularly if they are to overcome the real concerns expressed in the energy sector about these kinds of aggregated statistics. Indeed, these top-down views of what are complex patterns of social behaviour and transport use support the need for a better understanding of the causes of such changes – and, in doing so, drawing out implications about what can be done about them. But it is difficult to see that such concerns rule out the need for a top-down view of the complexity in which transport activity now takes place. Ultimately, a cross-national comparison of GTIs would provide a valuable top-down view of the linkages between transport and economic growth in different countries and could support more detailed bottom-up analyses needed to explain these long-term trends. Such analysis would have to take into account national characteristics such as physical geography, climate, economic activity, culture and population density – and could learn from existing analysis of energy intensity.

# Chapter 6

## The Policy Analogue: Transport Efficiency

*We suggest that copying, borrowing and pinching are widespread in the actual [policy] design process and that there are styles of policy analysis that could produce useful information for it.*

A. SCHNEIDER AND H. INGRAM, 'SYSTEMATICALLY PINCHING IDEAS: A COMPARATIVE APPROACH TO POLICY DESIGN', JOURNAL OF PUBLIC POLICY, VOL. 8, NO. 1, 1988, P.79

## 6.1 Introduction

Efficient transport can mean several things. Reducing the gross (mass) intensity could be identified with increasing aggregate 'transport efficiency', though by analogy with debates about the primary energy intensity, this has its limitations. At a more disaggregated level the concept is also not simple. Transport is not simply about physical movements, it is about money, time, effort, comfort, safety, reliability, habit, addiction and culture. There are a variety of ways in which individuals, households and firms could save time, money, effort and the physical movements involved in the use of transport services without losing any benefits. Not all journeys are as important as each other and not all goods need to be forwarded with the same speed. Several factors will already be preventing many journeys or goods movements which might take place were transport made easier, just as other factors are causing journeys to take place when they otherwise would not. Yet of the current journeys taking place, many of them could be made slightly or very differently and some of them even not at all. Walking and cycling are manifestly cheaper (in monetary terms) than any form of transport, yet they account for very little distance travelled, while initiatives such as car sharing or 'paratransit' reduce the cost of journeys per individual considerably.[129]

Where there is unnecessary movement, it is entirely reasonable to assume that without this the economy could function more productively, more healthily and less stressfully. In effect, sometimes reducing movement has the same effect as making steps to provide for it – such as building more road capacity – but without the same environmental and social costs.

There is a variety of strategic macroscopic pressures backing up the need to improve transport efficiency:

- pressure for greater economic competitiveness – to ensure that use of transport, as with the use of energy, capital, labour and other raw materials, is optimized subject to broad social cost-benefit criteria;
- pressure for enhanced social, welfare and safety policy – to enhance standards of living by increasing accessibility, reducing fear and road accidents and avoiding community severance and social isolation, by minimizing unnecessary consumer expenditure on poor-quality transport, particularly for those on low incomes, and by releasing capital that can be invested in a more profitable way (from a sustainability perspective); and
- pressure to improve the physical environment – to control the impacts of transport activity upon both the local environment (e.g. congestion and noise) and global environment (e.g. global climate instability and depletion of non-renewable resources).

This chapter develops one of the most difficult to understand, but potentially crucial concepts which comes out of the analogy with energy – 'transport efficiency'. Right away, it must be stressed that the story of energy efficiency *in practice* is not necessarily one that ought to be advocated for transport. Energy efficiency policy has gained many critics as well as supporters over the last two decades. However, the story of energy efficiency *in theory* – the analytical tools and concepts developed in the literature for assessing policy options – does seem to offer much to transport policy in the 1990s. Indeed

---

[129] See Vuchic, *Urban Public Transportation.* Paratransit is urban passenger road transport services available to specific groups of users or the public, but unlike traditional bus services, for example, is adaptable in its routing and scheduling to individual user desires in varying degrees.

many barriers to energy efficiency experienced in practice are not always generically the same as those that would appear to prevent greater transport efficiency. Although there are some central similarities between energy and transport, there are of course many more differences. This is a key point, as it suggests that the theoretical lessons which might be drawn from the energy efficiency experience may have very different practical trajectories if taken up in the transport sector.

## 6.2 UK energy efficiency

Chapter 3 has set out the broad development of UK energy efficiency policy. It illustrated that UK energy efficiency has developed in three broad phases.[130] It began in the mid 1970s as energy conservation, with an emphasis on preserving what were thought then to be scarce supplies of fuel. In the 1980s, there was a shift in emphasis towards the financial cost-effectiveness of energy efficiency. Recently, energy efficiency policy has become central to the government's aims of reducing the environmental impacts of fuel production and use, notably as a way of reducing greenhouse gas emissions and improving air quality.[131] As part of the UK's Strategy for Sustainable Development, the government maintains that a 20% improvement in energy efficiency in all energy sectors other than transport could be readily achieved by straightforward investments with paybacks within three years.[132] In the longer term, the technical potential for how much energy could be saved by the widespread application of current best-practice or readily identifiable future best-practice technology is even greater.

The 30% reduction in national energy intensity since 1960, noted in the previous chapter, has occurred against a complex background of structural economic changes away from energy-intensive industry, changes in the UK's fuel mix, and fluctuating energy prices. Evaluating the effects of government energy efficiency policy against this complex background is a difficult task. In 1987, the IEA's review of energy efficiency policies pointed out that:

---

[130] House of Commons Environment Committee, *Energy Efficiency in Buildings*, Vol. 1, HMSO, London, 1993.

[131] HMSO, *Climate Change: The UK Programme*, Cm 2427, HMSO, London, 1994.

[132] *Sustainable Development: The UK Strategy*.

The increase in energy prices and long standing trends towards increased productivity were the driving forces in bringing about these [energy efficiency] improvements but they were supplemented by government policies and programmes to promote energy conservation.[133]

A substantial review of UK energy efficiency programmes was undertaken in 1989 by the UK government's National Audit Office (NAO) – a body which monitors government spending. In 1989, the government calculated that over the period 1983–87, the decline in national UK energy intensity had, in effect, saved £2,290 million per year at 1983 prices.[134] However, it was not clear to what extent energy efficiency programmes had contributed to this improvement.

There are now a variety of well-documented reasons why energy efficiency is less than the economic optimum and experience with implementing demand management in the energy sector has highlighted a broad range of barriers to greater energy efficiency (Box 6.1).[135] These barriers send an important message out from the energy sector. The message is that it is not enough simply to identify which technical options are necessary to diversify and manage demand, but there is a role for a sound government-led implementation strategy to overcome some of the more intractable barriers to achieving greater sustainability in the use of energy.[136] There is now a valuable pool of knowledge in the UK and elsewhere on the problems of attempting to overcome this diverse range of barriers – knowledge which is potentially of great use to the transport sector. The UK government's attempts to implement energy efficiency policy have centred on overcoming these barriers via the three main strategies described in Chapter 3 (Box 3.1): information programmes; financial incentive programmes; and regulatory programmes.

[133] International Energy Agency, *Energy Conservation in IEA Countries*, OECD, Paris, 1987, p.8.
[134] National Audit Office, *National Energy Efficiency*, p. 7.
[135] See for example M. Grubb, 'Closing the End-use Efficiency Gap', in *Energy Policies and the Greenhouse Effect*, Vol.1: *Policy Appraisal*, Royal Institute of International Affairs, London, 1991. See also I. Christie and N. Ritchie, *Energy Efficiency: The Policy Agenda for the 1990s*, Policy Studies Institute, London, 1992.
[136] C. Hope and S. Owens, *Moving Forward: Overcoming the Obstacles to a Sustainable Transport Policy*, Professional Environmental Seminar Proceedings, Cambridge Environment Initiative, The White Horse Press, Cambridge, 1994.

The first UK information programme for energy conservation – the 'Save It' campaign – was introduced in the UK in December 1973 and was judged to have had little impact.[137] However, a variety of information programmes have continued to be a central feature of energy efficiency policy and have been carried out in conjunction with limited financial investment incentives. In general, information programmes are thought not to have been singularly successful, partly because their success is dependent upon the information being vivid, personalized, concrete and targeted to specific energy users and energy end-uses – criteria which were not often achieved.[138] Part of the reason for the failure of some early programmes was their tendency to focus upon behavioural conservation measures (e.g. turning down thermostats) rather than increased energy efficiency (e.g. investment in cavity insulation). For example, the UK 'Save It' campaign is remembered by people as implying the need to economize on comfort.[139] Exhortation measures alone are often not enough to encourage action.

The success of energy efficiency programmes has been hampered by energy consumers' fuzzy understanding of the concepts of energy and energy efficiency and by the difficulty dealing with the abstract nature of energy. People do not generally perceive that they buy energy, but rather that they buy light, petrol and heat.[140]

Financial investment incentives such as energy efficiency grants and loans are thought to have been marginally more successful than information programmes especially when they were used selectively to support the operations of the market. In general, there is no clear indication that grants were more effective than loans (and were presumably much more expensive), but there is evidence that integrated energy service programmes (co-ordinated packages of local authority-administered programmes and incentives from all the various

---

[137] In many senses energy conservation will have probably already given any transport corollary a bad name. W. Patterson in *The Energy Alternative*, Optima, London, 1990, recalls that one government publicity campaign exhorted people to 'SWITCH OFF SOMETHING – NOW!' and recounts 'One hapless Conservative Minister proposed that people save electricity by brushing their teeth in the dark'. It is not entirely out of the question that a transport efficiency message in the wrong hands could become 'STOP IT – NOW!'

[138] J.B. Robinson, 'The Proof of the Pudding: Making Energy Efficiency Work'.

[139] Department of Environment, *Attitudes to Energy Conservation in the Home*, p. 114.

[140] Ibid.

**Box 6.1 Barriers to improved energy efficiency**

*Lack of information and expertise among energy consumers*
- The concepts of energy and energy efficiency are not well understood by energy consumers.
- Energy used in private households can seem negligible compared with images of energy use by countries, governments, industries and other organizations.
- Links between domestic energy use and environmental damage are not well known.
- Less intensive industrial energy consumers typically have little understanding of energy flows within their industries.
- Energy consumption is effectively invisible, because most energy consuming systems and services do not directly report energy consumption on a frequent basis (the fuel gauge in the car is the most obvious exception).
- Consumers have a lack of confidence in new technologies or processes.

*Economic barriers*
- Energy costs are only a small proportion of total costs in many businesses and higher-income households (and thus receive little attention).
- The initial investments of time and effort into improving energy efficiency often deter people from acting. Energy management is not high on the agenda compared with increasing production, and unstable prices make it difficult to assess payback periods.
- Consumers expect energy efficiency investments to pay for themselves in 2–4 years, whereas the energy supply industries operate on longer time scales and lower rates of return.

*Institutional barriers*
- Energy supply is concentrated in a few large companies, whereas

*continued ...*

a great many small companies provide energy efficiency products and services. Energy sales are marketed more effectively than energy efficiency. The most energy-efficient products are often not readily available.
- The market is dominated by supply companies, with interests in increased sales (and only rarely an economic interest in promoting energy efficiency).
- Those who may pay for improving energy efficiency do not always get the benefits (as with the landlord-tenant relationship, where the landlord has little or no incentive to spend money on improving the property so as to reduce bills the tenant may pay).
- Capital expenditure in the public sector is more tightly controlled than running costs. Pricing policies for larger consumers can distort the market and declining bulk tariffs have proved a disincentive to energy efficiency.
- Energy users can sometimes be shielded from the full cost of energy (e.g. when energy costs are included in rent and when company cars are provided).

actors and organizations involved) have been most successful in overcoming many of the institutional and organizational barriers to improvements in energy efficiency that exist.[141]

Research suggests that a rational economic model of energy-consuming behaviour does not, on its own, adequately describe actual energy-using activities and investments and that there is little evidence of any direct link between attitudes towards energy use and actual energy-using behaviour.[142] In this respect, regulations and standards have been the most reliable and easiest methods of improving energy efficiency. Their conceptual significance, large impacts and relative ease of implementation mean that their use entails the minimum of effort in achieving energy efficiency improvements. However, within the energy sector it has been difficult to design regulations which receive a wide acceptance from the typically large number of interests affected –

---

[141] J.B. Robinson, 'The Proof of the Pudding: Making Energy Efficiency Work'.
[142] Ibid.

especially in the UK, where successive governments have rested a great deal of their energy policy (especially concerning demand) on assumptions about efficient markets and consumer sovereignty.[143] However, there is now a good understanding of why energy efficiency improvements are not always readily taken up – some of the well-documented and complex reasons have been described above. It is quite possible that the equivalent kinds of barriers to improving energy efficiency turn out to be very different in the transport sector. The energy efficiency experience is useful for thinking about how transport policy could overcome some of the barriers to more sustainable transport by promoting transport efficiency.

### 6.3 Transport efficiency: lessons from the energy sector

*Barriers to improved transport efficiency*
Travel decisions are complex, and for most journeys – and investments – criteria of environmental impact or perhaps even financial cost come low on the list. Most importantly, time is a major proportion of the 'generalized' costs of travel and plays a key role in shaping travel behaviour – the distances and frequencies of trips and choice of mode.[144] A switch to public transport, cycling or walking may often increase journey time. But several other factors influence travel choices, including: safety, personal security, and weather protection.

The idea that wasteful energy losses could be avoided through cost-effective good housekeeping measures was an attractive motivation for both propagators and receivers of the energy efficiency message – the idea of something for nothing. As long as behavioural change (e.g. ride sharing or switching to public transport) is perceived as a loss of either convenience, time or status, there is no clear consumer parallel of 'waste' in transport. Energy efficiency was not perceived by consumers to mean a loss of service or choice. For example, less energy could be used to achieve the same room temperature

---

[143] For a clear statement of the government's commitment to pro-market forces, anti-planning and anti-intervention energy policy see Department of Trade and Industry, *The Prospects for Coal: Conclusions of the Government's Coal Review*, HMSO, London, 1993.

[144] D.M. Newbery, 'Economic Principles Relevant to Road Pricing', *Oxford Review of Economic Policy*, Vol. 6, No. 2, 1990, pp.22–38.

and therefore the same result. Apart from encouraging modal-switching, improving transport's sustainability may partly require journeys to become shorter and less frequent – changes which at the moment could only be achieved at a loss of choice.

A number of barriers – analogous to those which prevent greater energy efficiency – are preventing society from operating at a higher level of transport efficiency (Box 6.2). Many of these barriers are directly analogous to those which exist in the energy sector.

So although there are strong macroeconomic grounds for improving transport efficiency, and the measures which are needed to diversify and manage demand are known, there are still considerable information, economic and institutional barriers which prevent improvements in national transport efficiency.

The existence of these complex barriers means that raising transport prices, even if politically feasible, is only one among many factors needed to improve transport efficiency.[145] Indeed, the fact that transport use has grown persistently despite relatively high fuel taxes throws doubt on the scope for politically feasible – or analytically justifiable – price rises to arrest demand growth. It is possible that direct pricing of transport use (e.g. road pricing) would have more psychological impact than rising fuel prices – psychological effects were an important factor in the energy transition and deserve further analysis in the context of transport.

In 1964, the UK government published a landmark study on the future of traffic in towns.[146] Three decades on, there have been many comprehensive reviews of options to diversify and manage the demand for transport in the UK as elsewhere. There is therefore no shortage of potential technical remedies and further options related to diversification and demand management and more alternatives, particularly technology-based, are still being generated (Box 6.3). However, it is now clear that no single measure – technological,

---

[145] P.B. Goodwin, 'A Review of New Demand Elasticities With Special Reference To Short and Long Run Effects of Price Changes', *Journal of Transport Economics and Policy*, Vol. XXVI, No. 2, May 1992, pp. 155–169. Evidence suggests that in the long run, pricing has a major effect on travel demand, though it is uncertain how political, psychological and institutional feedbacks from cumulative price increases would limit their contribution to managing overall demand. It is likely that any price increases would need to be supplemented with the backing of a full range of additional measures.

[146] HMSO, *Traffic in Towns*, HMSO, London, 1963.

**Box 6.2 Barriers to improved transport efficiency**


*Lack of information and expertise among transport users*
- The full transport implications and lifestyle changes that are involved when, for example, buying a house or taking a new job are complex.
- Car users typically lack information about public transport costs, times, routes and schedules.
- Apart from its contribution to the final price, the transport content of goods and services is invisible - they are 'hidden' factors of production.
- Public transport is perceived as less comfortable and of lower status than private travel.
- There is a lack of information on the health impacts of travel choices (e.g. driving stress) and confusion over some of the risks involved when walking or cycling.

*Economic barriers*
- The marginal cost of driving is small compared with other fixed costs.
- The price people pay for transport does not necessarily reflect its full social costs.
- Transport consumers have fast payback requirements (e.g. annual season tickets) so that investments aimed at reducing the length/ frequency of trips must often start to payback quicker than is feasible.
- Company cars users are shielded from the real costs of their car travel in terms of car purchase, fuel tax, insurance, servicing and company car parking. Step jumps in the miles-for-tax allowance system actually encourage unnecessary car travel.

*Institutional barriers*
- The funding of improvements and expansion to road infrastructure

*continued ...*

is divorced from the use of that infrastructure.

- Bus companies, taxi drivers, airlines and rail companies have no economic incentives to invest in measures which may reduce the need to travel by these modes.
- Decisions by land developers to build shops and facilities out of town.
- Employers' location decisions may take little account of the generalized transport costs which their prospective employees will face.
- Cars are potent status symbols - people are conditioned from childhood onwards to aspire to own and use a car, and to respect speed and acceleration.

fiscal or regulatory – will serve all the needs of a sustainable transport policy.[147] The challenge which planners and policy-makers are now facing is how to choose the best combination of measures from the options and alternatives put forward. This is not an easy task as there are still large political and economic uncertainties surrounding the various options, particularly urban road pricing. However, the optimal package of measures is likely to be the one which combines technological 'cures' as well as coupled behavioural and technological options for prevention as part of a co-ordinated supply and demand-side strategy to improve transport efficiency.

In addition there is a range of efficiency improvements which could also be made through behavioural change on the part of transport users. Box 6.4 outlines the kinds of policy options which the analogy with energy suggests might form part of a government strategy to overcome some of these barriers and improve transport efficiency.

There are a variety of ways in which more information could be put across to individuals and organizations simply and effectively to influence their travel and transport decisions. General information programmes could, for example, include campaigns to raise awareness of the issues and opportunities, backed up by specific measures to encourage financial and behavioural investments in

---

[147] Lowe, *Alternatives to the Automobile: Transport for Liveable Cities.*

**Box 6.3 Technical and structural options to improve transport efficiency**

*1. Options to reduce the overall demand for transport*
This category of measures is the most progressive and consequently requires high levels of behavioural change and technological substitution. Options include:

- land use planning to reduce journey lengths through greater integration of land use and transport planning measures;
- elimination of some journeys altogether by reducing or substituting for transport-based communication – teleworking, teleshopping, telelearning.

*2. Options to encourage diversification towards alternative carriers*
Much of the emphasis in past attempts to improve transport have focused on measures in this category, of which many there are many. Options include:

- land use planning measures to improve accessibility, rather than mobility, and encourage a shift from the private car towards either walking, cycling or public transport;
- improved facilities for pedestrians and cyclists;
- investment to improve quality and quantity of public transport (e.g. better passenger, route, and timetable information - transport informatics);
- traffic restrictions, bans and calming measures to reduce impacts and give more priority to other modes of transport.

*3. Options to make better use of existing modes and forms of transport*
Both technological and behavioural changes can achieve significant improvements in the use of existing modes/forms of transport. Options include:

- increased passenger vehicle occupancies (e.g. high occupancy vehicle lanes, ride sharing, reducing empty running in public

*continued ...*

> transport and increased occupancy rates);
> - spreading of peak demand through flexible working hours, staggered school hours and more freight movements at night;
> - increased freight transport efficiency (reducing empty journeys through increased backhauling and use of freight distribution and logistic centres);
> - smaller and lighter vehicles combined with traffic engineering measures to reduce congestion;
> - advanced travel information systems for public transport combined with restrictions on car use – speed and access controls.

improved transport efficiency.[148] Local advisory services could co-ordinate information on the range of opportunities for improved transport efficiency, perhaps acting as a contact point for businesses interested in supplying transport efficiency products and services. The energy experience indicates that transport audits, particularly in large organizations, may encourage changes towards transport efficiency. In addition, the audits could be backed up by a range of technical handbooks. Technical information could describe some of the opportunities there are for changing travel patterns – for example to and from work/school – and perhaps pointing out some of the difficulties which may have to be overcome in the use of new information and communications technologies. Indeed, for industry and commerce such handbooks could describe both the benefits and problems which employers and employees would encounter when establishing ride-sharing or teleworking schemes. Perhaps most importantly, training and education programmes could help to install firmly the concepts of transport efficiency for present and future transport users. Governments could promote transport management initiatives in the form of workshops, seminars, conferences and research projects, providing specific funds for training local and national policy-makers in the area of transport efficiency.

The lessons of energy efficiency indicate that government-led exhortation measures are rarely enough on their own to make individuals and organizations change their behaviour for long. However, the energy experience does indicate

---

[148] In one English county, Hampshire, a significant campaign of this sort to increase travel awareness was launched in 1994.

Box 6.4 Policy options to improve transport efficiency

*Information programmes*
- General campaigns, aimed at large audiences, informing travellers and freight managers of the needs and benefits of transporting themselves and their goods efficiently and emphasizing the transport content of goods and services.
- Transport audits – these could be done to increase awareness of the opportunities for greater efficiency both in the freight and passenger sectors.
- Technical handbooks – aimed at the public and organizations on the use of substitute information technologies and alternative transport technologies.
- Advisory services – would provide a co-ordinated point of contact and information for goods and services with the potential to reduce the need for transport.
- Training and education programmes – for school children, the public, organisations and for professionals in the transport field would help to get across the concept of sustainable transport.

*Financial investment incentives*
- Grants/loans – for example to encourage location and relocation to more accessible sites, purchase company mini-buses, purchase advanced communications technologies, or to employ a transport co-ordinator within the organization.
- Price incentives – to increase marginal cost of motorized travel, e.g. road pricing, increased fuel taxes, parking charges, reduction of tax allowances on company car travel and removal of 'step distortions', tax allowances for company bicycle travel, fuel and road tax exemptions for public transport operators.
- Tax allowances/exemptions for companies, providing what amount to packages of services which improve transport efficiency (e.g. vehicle leasing services, advanced telecommunications services, home delivery services and rural shops/amenities).

*continued ...*

> **Regulations and standards**
> - Where necessary, regulations targeted for example by journey purpose – e.g. work, education, shopping and leisure – could be introduced so that, for example schools and larger employers are encouraged to offer incentives for people to change their travel behaviour (similar, for example, to the Californian 'Commuter Program' which requires employers to offer incentives to reduce commuting by car).
> - Land use planning constraints to prevent urban sprawl and out-of-town developments, where services, employment and leisure activities are spread over large areas, too large for walking and cycling and not dense enough to support public transport.

that information programmes can provide a crucial role in persuading consumers to take up other opportunities such as grants/loans or voluntary standards. The energy efficiency experience also suggests that well-designed regulations (analogous to those governing energy efficiency standards in buildings or the US Corporate Average Fuel Efficiency (CAFE) standards) have the potential to be extremely effective in achieving transport efficiency goals. Such regulations could deal with specific types of transport end-uses, e.g. shopping, banking and some medical, work and education needs, or could focus on guidance for new settlement and land-use patterns.

Transport's close ties with lifestyles, industry and the economy will mean that transport efficiency policies need to be carefully integrated with economic and social objectives and will therefore take time to develop. Indeed, many of the policies for promoting transport efficiency could emerge as similar to those which were implemented in the energy sector in the wake of the 1973 energy crisis, but this time they are emerging from the multitude of concerns over transport impacts outlined in Chapter 2. Set against this, travel patterns are not just determined by individuals' decisions alone. A number of powerful and complex economic forces are also vested in maintaining the growth of transport demand. Human-powered forms of transport – walking and cycling – contribute little to GDP whereas motorized carriers, and cars in particular, do.

Transport efficiency serves multiple objectives – economic, environmental and social – and therefore has implications covering several different policy areas. Further research on the co-ordination of these related policy problems is needed, particularly with regard to potential conflicts of objectives. The energy-transport analogy suggests that further work to collate evidence of potential barriers to improved transport efficiency should be undertaken. When such work focuses on the behavioural aspects of transport usage, research in the energy sector suggests that a cross-national comparison of social activity, attitudes and travel choices towards transport use could provide valuable insights for the design of successful transport efficiency policies.

# Chapter 7

## The Futures Analogue: Planning Under Uncertainty

The prospect of roughly a doubling of total traffic on the UK's roads over the next 30 years has elicited unprecedented reactions to further significant traffic growth. Forecasting this far ahead is of course fraught with uncertainty, but nevertheless the National Road Traffic Forecasts are playing a strategic role in focusing minds on the possible long-term implications of incremental traffic growth. In fact, the NRTF have begun to feed back tangibly into transport thinking – initially outside government, and also now there are some signs from within. The result is that the forecasts have created a significant 'policy feedback', and even greater uncertainty surrounding the projection of UK transport over this period. The NRTF may well turn out to have been perhaps *the* major event in catalysing the transport transition which now looks to be underway in the UK.

This chapter aims to implant the basic culture of scenario analysis as it began to evolve in the energy sector during the 1970s into transport thinking by exploring two alternative 'top-down' scenarios of what could happen to the pattern of UK transport demand by 2025.[149] One represents a high-growth future – based on the Department of Transport's 1989 projections – and the other represents a low-growth future – developed by assuming a series of simple 'what if' changes relative to the high scenario which change the nature and structure of transport demand. The likelihood that such a low scenario is realized depends very much on the strengths and successes of any policy responses to manage the problems of transport growth.

---

[149] The scenarios developed are very basic in terms of the sophistication which can be used in such analyses – the intention here is only to suggest that they can be a useful tool in contemplating widely differing but internally and externally consistent futures.

## 7.1 New uncertainties for the analysis of transport futures in the UK

The transition towards demand management which is now underway in UK transport calls the traditional predict and provide approach to transport planning firmly and squarely into question. In turn, important new uncertainties have been added to the already colourful background of existing long-term planning uncertainty. These new uncertainties surround the emergence of new types of government and societal responses to both the real effects of actual transport increases and the psychological impacts of projected transport growth. Indeed, the NRTF have already had a considerable psychological impact on current transport thinking and could certainly never have taken into account the reactions they have invoked. Forecasting techniques such as the one used in the NRTF are not designed to take into account these broader types of uncertainty and under such conditions often become almost redundant.[150] Indeed the model used to produce the government's 1989 projections of traffic growth did not even take into account the feedback effects that traffic increases would have on demand through increased congestion – implicitly assuming that the relationship between road capacity and traffic volumes would not alter significantly. In the past, it is this sort of assumption which has led to the traditional criticism that such forecasts are used to legitimate further road improvements and expansion programmes which in turn have created further increases in road traffic – in much the same way that high energy predictions in the 1970s were used to legitimate government-led nuclear programmes in the UK.[151] The Department of Transport is currently reviewing its forecasting methodology in the light of such concerns.

The radically new environment surrounding the future direction which traffic and transport growth may take, calls for ways of contemplating a range of alternative futures to deal with the growing uncertainties and pressures within transport policy. In this sense, the scenario process – which does not attempt

---

[150] A.D. Pearman, 'Scenario Construction for Transport Planning', *Transportation Planning and Technology*, Vol. 12, No. 1, 1988, pp. 73–85 (cf. p.74). The NRTF have a low and a high projection (determined largely by GDP and fuel price) although these do not represent structural scenarios.

[151] On self-fulfilling transport forecasting see J.I. Gershuny, 'Transport Forecasting: Fixing the Future', in T. Whiston (ed.), *The Uses and Abuses of Forecasting*, Macmillan, London, 1979. On the supply approach to nuclear planning see W.C. Patterson, *Going Critical: An Unofficial History of British Nuclear Power*, Paladin, London, 1985.

to predict the future – represents a useful way of envisioning the range of possible outcomes under these kinds of uncertainty. In using scenarios as a tool for transport planning, the comfort of having a forecast is lost, but so too is the scepticism surrounding the accuracy of such unconditional forecasts.

## 7.2 Two alternative scenarios for the UK up to 2025

The aim here is to contrast two alternative views of how transport in the UK could develop up to 2025. A high-growth scenario ('NRTF') based on the mid-projection of the Department of Transport's 1989 NRTF is contrasted with a low-growth scenario ('Response') constructed in terms of feasible 'what if' changes in the pattern of transport demand and use.

Each of the scenarios can be described in terms of a set of overall passenger km, freight tkm and carrier km demand patterns, from which the aggregate GMMs and GTIs for each scenario can in turn be constructed (against background assumptions of changes in carrier mass productivities). The aim under each scenario is to present an overall picture of how the pattern of transport demand evolves, expressed in terms of modal splits, GMMs and GTIs. The midpoint of forecast GDP contained in the 1989 NRTF is used as an exogenous variable and the UK car population is assumed to reach its mid-forecast of 33 million (57 cars per 100 people) by 2025.

*NRTF scenario*
This scenario explicitly uses the predictions made by the Department of Transport's NRTF model to construct an overall picture of trends in transport activity up to 2025. As a first approximation, the interaction between the road traffic forecasts and trends in other modes is assumed to be negligible.[152] The NRTF model does not go as far as predicting the net amount of passenger or freight transport, but this can be done by taking observed long-run trends in carrier occupancies into account. An implicit estimate has therefore to be made of net road and non-road based passenger and freight movements implied in the NRTF. The calculation of the GMM takes into account the long-term

---

[152] As a first approximation and because of their relatively small and diminishing contribution to overall transport demand, rough estimates for changes in the demand for other modes not forecast by the NRTF – rail, water and air – are made based on previous trends.

projected trends in carriers, unladen masses and in particular the continuation of trends in unladen masses of cars and HGVs (see Appendix).

The sort of world in which the NRTF scenario may come true is one where strategic national demand management initiatives – of any kind – do not emerge. New road building and upgrading of classified roads would continue to be actively pursued at present rates, and public and political consensus on road pricing would not have been reached. This world would also be more probable if the marginal cost of car travel remained significantly unaltered in real terms, perhaps because small real increases in fuel prices would be more than outweighed by improvements in vehicle fuel efficiency. The freight side of this NRTF world is more credible with the vigorous development of trans-European road networks into and out of the UK facilitating a major expansion of UK trade. This would have implications for manufacturing and employment throughout the economy, encouraging further significant increases in average haul lengths which perhaps more than offset the slight shift to lighter, higher-value goods.

*Response scenario*
This basis of the Response scenario is an analysis of a series of detailed changes in several key parameters which have an effect on the value of GTI, including changes in the occupancies, modal splits, unladen masses and absolute levels of transport for each carrier (Table 7.1).

The response scenario assumes only a modest drop of 5% in overall passenger and tonne kilometres compared with the NRTF case. The focus of the scenario is primarily to explore the impact of the kinds of diversity and carrier efficiency measures described in Box 6.3. The Response scenario therefore represents a hypothetical, but reasonable, view of some radical developments in transport structures, but not overall net transport activity, compared with the NRTF scenario. The sort of world which makes this scenario more credible would perhaps be something like the following. The strategic national demand management ethic which started in the early 1990s grows over the period and begins to have a measurable effect on overall patterns of transport demand. By 2010, no new significant road expansion programmes are planned. Car ownership continues as forecast in the NRTF, but as a result of the successful implementation of urban and motorway road pricing – which significantly

**Table 7.1 Response scenario: effect of 'what if' changes on GTI relative to NRTF 2025**

| Changes relative to NRTF scenario 2025 | % reduction in GTI |
|---|---|
| 22% Modal shift from cars to 3% walk, 6% cycle, 4% motorcycle, and 9% bus | 6.7 |
| 15% Modal shift from HGV to 2% pipe, 2% ship, 11% rail | 4.2 |
| 20% Increase in mean occupancy of passenger trains (to 134 persons) | 1.0 |
| 10% Increase in mean occupancy of cars (to 1.65 persons) | 3.1 |
| 60% Increase in freight mean occupancy of LGV (to 0.31 tonnes) | 3.3 |
| 10% Increase in mean occupancy of HGV (to 6.6 tonnes) | 3.1 |
| 10% Reduction in the unladen mass of car (to 1.0 tonnes) | 3.1 |
| 10% Reduction in the unladen mass of HGV (to 10.9 tonnes) | 3.1 |
| 5% Reduction in income elasticity of passenger movements (to 0.37) | 2.0 |
| 5% Reduction in income elasticity of freight movements (to 0.83) | 3.0 |
| *Sum of all changes* | *32.6* |

Note: The feasibility of this set of changes was chosen under the assumption that relative ease of small changes in the four main types of options to reduce GTI occurred in the following order - from most feasible to most difficult changes: occupancies; modal splits; unladen carrier masses; overall passenger or freight elasticities. Starting in 1991, the final intensity is reached in 2025 by allowing the transition to the above configuration to be a succession of linear changes in each variable. In other words the rate of advancement towards the target intensity is constant.

increases the marginal cost of road travel – the kilometres driven per year per car drop from 17,000 in 1992 to 12,000 in 2025 (a level last observed in 1952). Participation in transport efficiency programmes grows rapidly including: work and school-based incentive schemes to encourage higher vehicle occupancies; and telecommunications services which substitute some working, shopping and personal journeys. In addition there is considerable psychological impact as cyclists and pedestrians are formally favoured over other road users while concessions for quiet and light motorcycles are also explicitly made. Bus services benefit from new information technologies improving routing, scheduling and flexibility, while continued advances in freight logistics and technological achievements in new materials and lighter vehicles as well as combined road/rail transport all help to reduce overall mass movements in the freight sector.

Table 7.2 shows the pattern of net transport demand and carrier movements for each of the two scenarios relative to 1992.

The Response scenario has been deliberately constructed to maintain almost the same level of net movement: there is a slackening of passenger and freight income elasticities of only around 5% compared with those of the NRTF scenario (total passenger km and freight are very similar in both scenarios in 2025 – Table 7.2). People and goods are not travelling much less in the Response scenario, they are just doing it differently. Hence, although the Response scenario involves significant behavioural changes on the part of transport users, it does not represent radical cultural change, or necessarily a lower bound. Under both scenarios, increases in both passenger and freight movements are projected to be roughly linear in time.

The Response scenario is radically different from the NRTF scenario. Indeed, it was designed to push the limits of credibility of what could be feasible changes in modal splits by 2025. For example, it is just possible that the cycle population in the UK would double to 32 million by the end of the period, which would translate the massive increase in cycling into an increase in kilometres cycled per person per week from 6 in 1992 to 42 in 2025. The decline in personal car use resulting from these changes and the increased occupancy noted above is at odds with most analyses of evolving car use. For the motor cycling switch to occur, the motor cycle population would, for example, have to increase fivefold (from 690,000 to 3,450,000 in 2025) and usage double.

The changes in the pattern of freight goods moved by 2025 also appear only just within the bounds of credibility – particularly for goods moved by train and pipe, both of which increase dramatically under this scenario. Train activity more than trebles from 16 btkm in 1992 to 59 btkm in 2025. Although this reflects goods movements by train keeping a similar proportion of overall goods movement in the two years, it essentially involves increasing goods moved by train by an amount equivalent to half the existing road freight in 1992. Pipe transfers also increase dramatically from 11 btkm in 1992 to 28 btkm in 2025. This would require belt or propulsion systems to be used for goods other than bulk liquids and gases, which is certainly technologically possible.

## Table 7.2 NRTF and Response scenarios: net activities and carrier movements relative to 1992

| | 1992 | NRTF 2025 | Response 2025 | % increase Response/NRFT |
|---|---|---|---|---|
| *BPKM* | | | | |
| Walk | 25 | 25 | 51 | 103 |
| Pedal cycles | 5 | 5 | 68 | 1217 |
| Motor cycles | 5 | 6 | 51 | 747 |
| Car/taxi | 585 | 953 | 679 | -29 |
| Bus/coach | 43 | 26 | 115 | 344 |
| Train | 38 | 38 | 36 | -5 |
| Air | 5 | 10 | 9 | -5 |
| All modes | 706 | 1063 | 1009 | -5 |
| | | | | |
| *BTKM* | | | | |
| LGV | 5 | 16 | 15 | -5 |
| HGV | 121 | 342 | 260 | -24 |
| Train | 16 | 8 | 59 | 674 |
| Water | 55 | 74 | 77 | 4 |
| Pipeline | 11 | 22 | 28 | 24 |
| All modes | 209 | 462 | 439 | -5 |
| | | | | |
| *Billion carrier kilometres* | | | | |
| Pedal-cycles | 5 | 5 | 68 | 1217 |
| Motor-cycles | 5 | 5 | 46 | 747 |
| Car/taxi | 335 | 635 | 411 | -35 |
| Bus/coach | 5 | 4 | 10 | 122 |
| Train | 0.35 | 0.35 | 0.27 | -24 |
| Air | 0.10 | 0.18 | 0.17 | -5 |
| | | | | |
| *Billion carrier kilometres* | | | | |
| LGVs | 37 | 83 | 49 | -41 |
| HGVs | 28 | 57 | 39 | -31 |
| Train | 0.03 | 0.02 | 0.12 | 674 |
| Water | 0 | 0 | 0 | 4 |
| Pipeline | – | – | – | – |
| | | | | |
| *Total* | *65* | *140* | *89* | *-37* |

Figure 7.1 compares how the passenger and freight modal splits evolve in the future under each of the scenarios. In each case the modal split is shown as a continuation of the trend in modal split actually observed since 1952.

In the NRTF scenario there is a steady increase in the proportion of passenger travel by car and accompanying decreases in the proportion of travel by all other modes. Similarly, the evolution of freight transport modal share in the NRTF scenario is dominated by the growth of HGV activity at the expense of other modes.

Under the Response scenario, modal shares for non-car-based passenger transport begin to increase steadily. This is in direct contrast to the NRTF scenario. The result is a gradual squeezing of the car's share of passenger transport and an increase in both walking, cycling and public transport. Whereas road freight movements continue to increase their overall share of all freight transport under NRTF, the Response scenario suppresses this trend by increasing the modal shares of non-road freight. The result is a 15% decrease in the modal share of HGV freight compared with the NRTF scenario in 2025.

The full picture of transport activity under each scenario can be constructed by combining the net activity for each scenario with its modal split profile over the period. This can be done by applying the GMM measure developed in Chapter 5 which aggregates complex patterns of transport activity into a single measure. The GMMs resulting from the two scenarios are shown in Figure 7.2

The figure shows that there is now a significant difference between the GMMs of the two scenarios by the end of the period. GMM under NRTF is nearly one-third higher than it is under the Response scenario. Even the Response scenario has a significant growth in GMM of around 50% compared with 1992.

GTIs for each of the two scenarios can now be constructed by combining GMM with forecast GDP. The Department of Transport estimates that over the forecast period GDP will increase at a constant rate of between 2 and 3% per year, i.e. 2.5% exponentially throughout the period. The evolution of GTI for each scenario can be constructed by combining the GMMs and the forecasts for GDP (Figure 7.3).

There is a significant difference in the evolution of GTI for each scenario – down to 2.5 tkme per £1 GDP in the NRTF scenario and down, even further, to 1.8 tkme/£1 GDP in the Response case. In contrast to the continued upward trend in GTI to the present, both the NRTF and the Response scenarios imply a

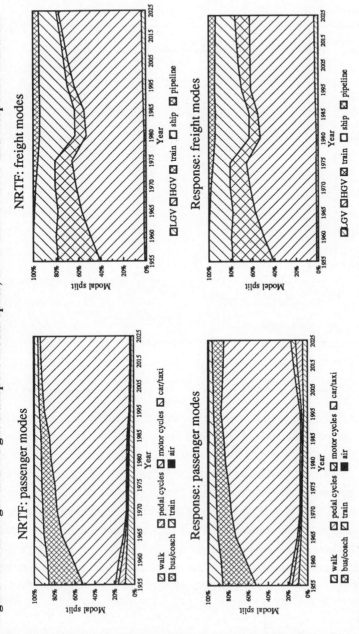

# Figure 7.1 Passenger and freight transport modal splits, 1955–2025: NRTF and Response scenarios

Source: the author.

Note: a change in the definition of waterborne transport (in 1976) dominates what otherwise would have been a steady increase in the proportion of HGV freight compared with all other freight modes.

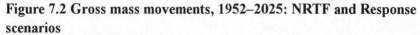

**Figure 7.2 Gross mass movements, 1952–2025: NRTF and Response scenarios**

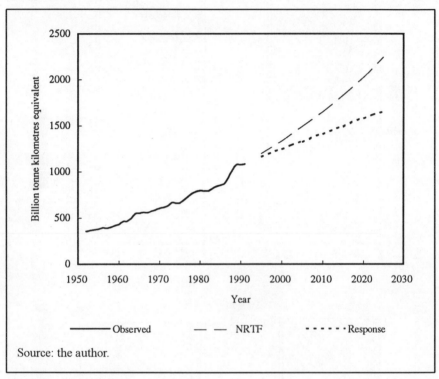

significant downturn in the growth of transport intensity. This is a key point. Since the government and other groups consider the NRTF forecasts higher than could be sustainably, or feasibly, accommodated (chapter 2), it is likely therefore that GTI will not be higher than this. The NRTF scenario's GTI therefore represents a good upper bound for the evolution of GTI. This strongly suggests that UK GTI will have peaked somewhere around the early 1990s – given the predicted increases in GDP.[153] The Response scenario represents a significantly lower GTI and involves some significant changes in the pattern of transport demand – changes which could only come about by a combination of

---

[153] Of course, historically, the growth of UK GDP has not been exponential – in fact it has been almost linear since the early 1950s. The deflection away from long-term trends in GTI shown in Figure 7.3 is reduced significantly – to a levelling off – by assuming linear growth in GDP, instead of exponential.

## Figure 7.3 Gross transport intensity, 1952–2025: NRTF and Response scenarios

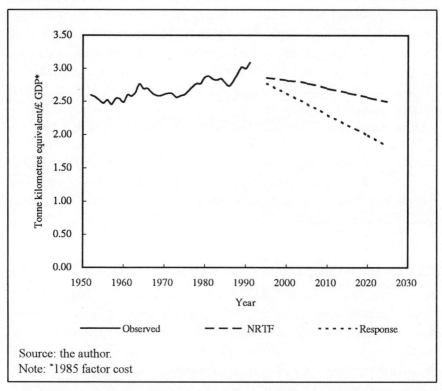

Source: the author.
Note: *1985 factor cost

radical changes in public attitudes towards driving, government's willingness to sponsor interventionist and regulatory policy initiatives and individuals' travel behaviour (though not overall volume). The contrast between the observed trends over the last forty years and the two future scenarios is stark, particularly in terms of implied income elasticities. Total passenger transport income elasticity drops from the long-term 1.05 as previously observed to 0.42 in the NRTF case, whilst total freight transport elasticity drops from 1.01 to 0.88.[154]

---

[154] Department of Transport, *National Road Traffic Forecasts (Great Britain) 1989*, paras 11/73. The NRTF are based mainly on past trends in the relationship between traffic and income which are forecast to continue. The elasticity of freight tonne km to GDP is assumed to be unity throughout the period – but clearly implies a considerable drop in overall freight income elasticity when changes in other modes are taken into account.

This simple top-down scenario analysis of trends in future UK transport begins to fulfil the need for a more strategic approach to transport planning, but is only the first step in a range of exploratory analyses which ought to be carried out. Since most policy measures implicitly assume interaction between the various transport modes and transport carriers and since environmental constraints operate across the whole transport sector, it is important that inter-modal and cross-carrier comparative analysis becomes a familiar part of national transport planning.

The method used to generate the Response scenario through a series of incremental 'what if' changes from the NRTF pictures of the future is a useful way of contemplating an uncertain future. Once the range of possibilities has been explored in more detail, there remains the important task of combining the transport forecasts with changes in the environmental and social problems which transport causes.

### 7.3 Conclusions: transport in macroeconomic transition

For the foreseeable future, GMM is set to continue rising in the UK as a result of further increases in road traffic. Only significant and rapid techno-logical or behavioural changes would curb the increased environmental and social impacts that such growth would otherwise cause. While passenger and freight tonne kilometres look set to continue increasing, the way this activity is distributed among available modes and technologies can make a considerable difference to the overall level of GMM, and therefore to overall environmental impacts – as demonstrated in the Response scenario.

However, while overall transport activity will continue to increase sig-nificantly, it is likely that this will not be at a rate which keeps pace with economic growth. For the long-term observed growth in GTI to continue, traffic levels would have to be double the NRTF predictions. The sudden downturn in GTI under the NRTF scenario, if realized, represents a significant departure from long-term trends in the relationship between transport demand and GDP and suggests that significant structural changes in the role of transport in the economy are set to occur. In some senses this notion has been implicit in the NRTF since they were introduced in 1989 – when GDP is forecast to increase exponentially while traffic movements (the bulk of transport) are expected to grow just linearly in time. It also comes as no surprise when the history of UK national primary energy intensity – which peaked in 1860 – is taken into account.[155] While the primary energy intensity has been declining steadily since late Victorian times, the demand for transport has continued to follow trends in GDP. At some stage – and this looks now to be sometime around the end of this century – UK GTI may well reach its turning point.

A wide range of policy options and responses to the social and environmental problems of transport are now being considered in the UK and elsewhere. Amidst the confusion and conflicts between one option and another, GMM offers a useful indicator for monitoring overall progress towards more sustainable transport and at a microscopic level gives new meaning to the expression 'travelling light'. There are many measures for reducing GMM – from radical options such as stabilization of passenger kilometres and freight tonne kilometres to easier options such as increasing average carrier occupancies – many of which carry significant environmental and social benefits. There are also several strategies to back up such measures. In the long term, raising the marginal price of transport will certainly help, although this is not likely on its own to be successful. Specific government measures such as those proposed in chapter 6 will also be needed to overcome some of the barriers to sustainable transport.

What is clear, however, is that modal shifts and efficiency improvements have the potential to significantly reduce the environmental impacts of transport and accelerate the decline of GTI.

Implementing the spirit of sustainability in the transport sector can be viewed as either a threat or as an opportunity. As a threat, it suggests constraints on consumer choice, personal freedoms and access, and higher transport costs. As an opportunity, it suggests an innovative transport future where the analogy with energy gives fresh meanings to some old solutions. The energy-transport analogy provides many fruitful avenues and experiences relevant to the search for economic and environmental harmony on the road to more sustainable mobility.

---

[155] See W.S. Humphrey and J. Stanislaw, 'Economic Growth and Energy Consumption in the UK, 1700–1975', *Energy Policy*, Vol. 7, No. 1, 1979, pp. 29–42. UK energy intensity peaked in 1860 at around 1.6 tonnes of oil equivalent (toe)/£1000 GDP to its present level of around 0.5 toe/£1000 GDP.

# Appendix

**Estimation of parameters in method to calculate gross mass movements**

The method for calculating GMM requires data which are not readily available and which therefore have to be estimated. Table A1 summarizes the different estimates of 'typical' unladen carrier masses which are needed to construct GMM.[156]

In estimating, for example, the typical unladen mass of a bus, there are large uncertainties. The designs of buses have changed dramatically over the last five years towards lighter and smaller vehicles. Buses have a long service life, however, and so the effects of the 1980 and 1985 Bus Deregulation Acts for instance (implicitly encouraging smaller vehicles) have not all been observed yet. Even some of the older and larger bus and coach stock are being modernized and reused. A double decker bus has 97 seats and the average single coach will hold around 70 people. The smaller town buses can carry 30 passengers. The 'typical' bus is assumed to carry 60 passengers and have an unladen mass of 7 tonnes.

A sensitivity analysis shows the effects of this kind of uncertainty on the final value of GMM for each parameter and therefore helps to establish the parameters where uncertainty has the most impact on the overall value of GMM.

**Treatment of uncertainty in estimation of unladen carrier masses**

Two types of uncertainty enter into the estimations of the average mass of unladen carriers:

(i) the values of some of the parameters may have varied significantly over the period of calculation – for example, as the law has permitted larger

---

[156] For full details of this method see Peake, *Cross-Sector Policy Research: Insights from the UK Energy and Transport Sectors.*

**Table A1 Values of unladen carrier masses (tonnes), ranges of uncertainty, and sensitivities**

| Carrier | Central Values | Units | Range (%)* | Sensitivity** |
|---|---|---|---|---|
| Person | 0.05 | tonnes | 50 | 1.9 |
| Cycle | 0.02 | tonnes | 20 | 0.002 |
| Motor cycle | 0.1 | tonnes | 30 | 0.02 |
| Car | 1.0 | tonnes | 30 | 10.6 |
| Bus | 7.0 | tonnes | 50 | 1.8 |
| Passenger train | 250 | tonnes | 30 | 3.6 |
| Plane | 60 | tonnes | 20 | 0.09 |
| LGV† | 1.5 | tonnes | 30 | 1.8 |
| HGV‡ | 4 | tonnes | 90 | 11.0 |
| Freight train | 745 | tonnes | 40 | 0.7 |
| Ship | 2130 | tonnes | 90 | 3.1 |
| Ship loads | 2000 | tonnes | 30 | -1.0 |

\* The range of possible values for the parameters lie within ± R% of the estimated value.
\*\* Maximum change in the value of GMM for 1991 as a result of a 1% change in the value of the parameter coupled with the range of uncertainty.
† Light Goods Vehicle (less that 3.5 tonnes gross weight).
‡ Heavy Goods Vehicle (greater than 3.5 tonnes gross weight).

HGVs on the road, the unladen mass and payload of an average HGV have increased; and
(ii) values of certain parameters are not well known – e.g. the average mass of unladen ships (their 'light displacement tonnage') is difficult to estimate.

A sensitivity analysis was carried out on a set of preliminary results (using static values for all parameters) to estimate the effects of changing the values of each of the parameters within probable minimum to maximum ranges (which are related to the two types of uncertainty involved, Table A1).

The sensitivity analysis indicates that gross mass movement is most sensitive to the values chosen for the unladen masses of cars and HGVs. GMM is around three times more sensitive to changes in these parameters than it is to changes in any of the others. An increase in the assumed average load on a ship decreases the value of gross mass movement and as such is represented as negative.

To gain a more accurate picture of the changes in annual gross mass movements over the period 1952–92 a detailed investigation of changes in car and HGV unladen carrier masses over the period was carried out (rather than just using the values in Table A1 unchanged over the whole period). The results of this analysis are shown in graphical forms in Figures A1 and A2. This analysis reduces the range of values for these parameters (the residual uncertainty associated with each of the data points shown in Figures A1 and A2 is estimated to be +/-5%). In the case of cars, the original estimate of unladen mass was very close to that obtained from a more detailed study, whereas significantly different results emerged from the HGV study. In the data presented in this report, the masses of cars and HGVs were therefore allowed to vary over the period according to the trends shown in Figures A1 and A2. The values of all other parameters used to calculate gross mass movements were held constant over the period 1952–92, as listed in Table A1.

*Unladen mass of a car*
Figure A1 shows the results of the analysis of changes in unladen mass of cars over the period 1952–92. A linear interpolation between four sample points is plotted. In comparison with the previous estimate of the uncertainty in the unladen mass of a car (1000 kg +/- 30% for the maximum change over the period 1952–92 – see Table A1), the range indicated by the sample points is 1000 kg + 10%. The remaining uncertainty in each of the four sample points is estimated to be around 5% which takes into account the fact that not all cars were included in the analysis, and certain types of cars are used more than others. A linear interpolation between the points (rather than some form of regression analysis) therefore gives an accurate estimation of the trend in unladen masses over the period.

*Unladen mass of an HGV*
The unladen mass of HGVs in four sample years are plotted in Figure A2 with a linear interpolation between them. The unladen mass rises fourfold over the period. In 1952, 95% of heavy goods vehicle kilometrage was due to

*Appendix*

**Figure A1  Changes in unladen mass of 'average' UK car: 1952–1992**

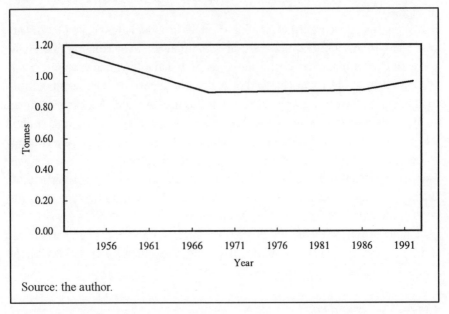

Source: the author.

vehicles equal to or less than 5 tonnes unladen mass. By 1991 the proportion of vehicle kilometres attributed to vehicles of unladen mass equal to or less than 5 tonnes had fallen to around 20%.[157]

The original estimate of the range of uncertainty for the unladen masses (Table A1) was not high enough; this calculation has revealed the 1992 estimate to be 120% greater than the original estimate, 30% greater than was thought possible (the results for the early part of the period are in line with Tupule's 1972 study of HGV use in the UK).[158]

[157] Department of Transport, *Survey of Road Goods Transportation*, HMSO, London, 1992.
[158] A.H. Tupule, *Trends in Freight in Great Britain*, Road Research Laboratory Report LR 429, Bracknell, 1972.

## Figure A2 Changes in unladen mass of 'average' UK HGV: 1952–1992

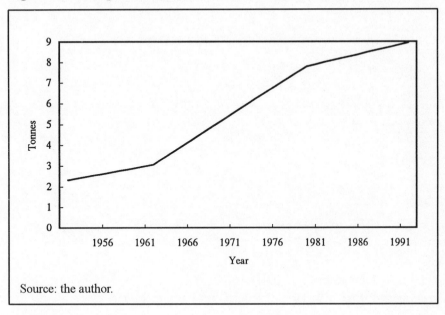

Source: the author.